What Are They Saying About the Formation of Pauline Churches?

Richard S. Ascough

PAULIST PRESS
New York/Mahwah, N.J.

Cover design by Jim Brisson

Library of Congress Cataloging-in-Publication Data

Ascough, Richard S.
    What are they saying about the formation of Pauline churches? / Richard S. Ascough.
        p.   cm.
    Includes bibliographical references.
    ISBN 0-8091-3768-2 (alk. paper)
    1. Pauline churches. 2. Christian communities—Mediterranean Region. 3. Bible. N.T. Epistles of Paul—Criticism, interpretation, etc. 4. Bible. N.T. Acts—Criticism, interpretation, etc. 5. Mediterranean Region—Church history. I. Title.
BS2545.P47A83   1998
270.1—dc21   97-32986
                                                                                CIP

Published by Paulist Press
997 Macarthur Boulevard
Mahwah, New Jersey 07430

Printed and bound in the
United States of America

Contents

Preface

My appreciation for Paul and his social world has come to me from many sources throughout my academic career. Of particular note, both Leif Vaage and B. Hudson McLean have given me much food for thought throughout many discussions together. Colleagues and fellow students at the Toronto School of Theology have been challenging dialogue partners, especially Alicia Batten, Caroline Whelan-Donaghey, Robert Derrenbacker, John McLaughlin and Tyler Williams. My involvement with the teenagers of "Triniteens" has challenged my understanding of Paul and his social world on a completely different level. My Doktorvater, John S. Kloppenborg, has been most helpful, both in my intellectual development and in putting this book together. He was a sounding board for many of my ideas and has diligently read various drafts of this book, making many helpful suggestions and corrections throughout. Of course any shortcomings remain my own.

Generous financial support has been granted to me during the writing of this book and the associated larger project of my Ph.D. dissertation from the following sources: a three-year fellowship from the Social Sciences and Humanities Research Council of Canada, four years of Catholic Biblical Association Memorial Stipends, the John M. Kelly Award from the Toronto School of Theology and a number of Wycliffe College bursaries. I am most grateful for all of these as they have allowed me the freedom to focus my attention on the immediate project at hand.

Finally, my most heartfelt thanks belong to my wife Mary-Lynne and my daughter Hannah, both of whom have provided familial stimulus that has refreshed me for continued academic study. It is to them that I dedicate this work, with love.

Abbreviations

ABD	*The Anchor Bible Dictionary,* 6 vols., ed. D. N. Freedman. New York: Doubleday, 1992.
ANRW	*Aufstieg und Niedergang der römischen Welt,* ed. H. Temporini and W. Hasse. Berlin: de Gruyter, 1972—
BARev	*Biblical Archaeology Review*
CBQ	*Catholic Biblical Quarterly*
CIJ	*Corpus Inscriptionum Iudaicarum*
CIL	*Corpus Inscriptionum Latinarum*
CIRB	*Corpus Inscriptionum Regni Bosporani*
CP	*Classical Philology*
EPRO	Études préliminaires aux religions orientales dans l'Empire romain
ExpTim	*Expository Times*
HSCP	*Harvard Studies in Classical Philology*
HTR	*Harvard Theological Review*
IG	*Inscriptiones Graecae*
ILS	*Inscriptiones Latinae Selectae*
Int	*Interpretation*
JAC	*Jahrbuch für Antike und Christentum*
JBL	*Journal of Biblical Literature*
JECS	*Journal of Early Christian Studies*
JEH	*Journal of Ecclesiastical History*
JRH	*Journal of Religious History*
JRS	*Journal of Roman Studies*
JSNT	*Journal for the Study of the New Testament*

JSNTSup *Journal for the Study of the New Testament* Supplement
         Series
JTS   *Journal of Theological Studies*
LEC   Library of Early Christianity
LXX   Septuagint
MTZ   *Münchner theologische Zeitschrift*
NewDocs *New Documents Illustrating Early Christianity,* 7 vols., ed.
         G. H. K. Horsely and S. R. Llewelyn. North Ryde:
         Macquarrie University Press, 1981–95
NovT   *Novum Testamentum*
NovTSup Novum Testamentum Supplements
NTS   *New Testament Studies*
RAC   *Reallexikon für Antike und Christentum,* 10 vols., ed.
         T. Klauser. Stuttgart: Hiersemann, 1950–78
RB   *Revue biblique*
SBLASP   Society of Biblical Literature Abstracts and Seminar Papers
SBLSBS   Society of Biblical Literature: Sources for Biblical Study
*SIG*³   *Sylloge Inscriptionum Graecarum*
SNTSMS   Society for New Testament Studies Monograph Series
TAPA   *Transactions of the American Philological Association*
TSK   *Theologische Studien und Kritiken*
TZ   *Theologische Zeitschrift*
VC   *Vigiliae christianae*
WUNT   Wissenschaftliche Untersuchungen zum Neuen Testament
ZWT   *Zeitschrift für wissenschaftliche Theologie*

Introduction

It is now a well-established assumption within New Testament studies that the church did not develop in a vacuum. As with any institution it drew upon its surrounding culture(s) for models on which to base itself. Over the years scholars have proposed a number of different analogous institutions which might have been the basis for the formation of Paul's churches. This book surveys the scholarly literature which examines the different models available in the Greco-Roman period for understanding how Paul's early Christian groups structured their communities: synagogues, philosophical schools, the mysteries[1] and voluntary associations. Emphasis is placed on individual scholars, their use of a model, the literary and archaeological data which they use and the data from the Pauline corpus which they emphasize.

While many scholars recognize the complexity of the ancient urban city and the need to acknowledge multiple influences on emerging Christianity, I will, for convenience and practicality, discuss each scholar under the rubric which they see as being *most* predominant.[2] What is at issue is not what Paul himself would have been most familiar with, but what the groups which he formed in the Greco-Roman urban centers would have looked like, both to those who attended and to those on the outside. With what would both groups have most naturally associated the Pauline churches?[3] Thus, there will be a two-pronged approach evident in the works summarized in the following chapters: how Pauline groups constituted themselves (consciously or unconsciously) *and* how Christian groups appeared to outsiders.[4]

E. A. Judge has provided a strong and consistent voice calling for the study of the context of Pauline Christianity. In an article published in 1960 he wrote,

> We need to know not only who they were, and what relation they had as a group to the social structure of their own communities, but what they existed for as a group, what activities they engaged in, and what their contemporaries would have made of them. This is, of course, purely a question of external appearances and social function. The theological rationale of the church is not our concern. (Judge 1960a:8)

Some twenty years later Judge still had need to write that, "[u]ntil the work of mapping out their social identity and behaviour has been developed much further in juxtaposition with the conventions and practices of contemporary society, we are in no position to say who or what the first Christians were" (1980:213; cf. 216). This book is an attempt to map out what has been done until now as a way of determining both where we stand as New Testament exegetes and where we need to go in the future.

To date there has not been a sustained attempt to map out the scholarly discourse in the area of Pauline community formation. The impetus for this particular book came early on in my doctoral studies from my reading of **Wayne A. Meeks's** *The First Urban Christians* (1983). In that book Meeks examines four models of community formation: the household, voluntary associations, synagogues and philosophical schools (1983:74–84). Although Meeks presents a brief sketch which fits his purpose, I decided that a more detailed survey of these models would better suit the beginning student of early church formation. My search for this more adequate survey revealed that none existed; thus I decided to draw together some of the strands myself. In addition, since the publication of Meeks's book, there has been a considerable output of articles and books which discuss the possible models for early Christian communities. However, none, to my knowledge, gives the overarching summary of scholarship which this book attempts.

In this book we are attempting to look into the social history of the early church as opposed to the sociological analysis of the early church. While this separation of approaches is somewhat artificial (see Scroggs 1980:167–68), it will be helpful to keep in mind that we are only examining one-half of what many scholars are attempting when looking at the New Testament in its social context. For a succinct account of various sociological analyses, see *Caroline Osiek, What Are They Saying About the Social Setting of the New Testament?* (1992).

This book is meant to be introductory and is aimed at the beginning student and the interested lay person. For this reason I have avoided technical discussions as much as possible. Of necessity this has meant some simplification in the nuances of the arguments of various authors. The interested reader would do well to read the works described herein in order to gain an appreciation of the full impact of the arguments. For the most part I have also limited this survey to works written in English or available in English translation, again with the intended readership in mind.

Summary of the Contents of the Book

The first chapter considers the ancient synagogue as a model for Pauline community formation. The synagogue was an organization of Jews who met together for times of worship, either in a household or a special building. The chapter begins by considering the evidence from Acts that presents Paul preaching first to the members of synagogues in each city, and, when rejected, turning to the Gentiles. This presentation in Acts raises a number of important issues for the study of early church formation that we will consider in turn: the nature of synagogue organization, the extent of Jewish proselytism in the first century and the existence (or lack) of proselytes and God-fearers attached to the synagogue. A decision on each of these issues will affect how one understands the relationship of the church and the synagogue in the first century. Finally, we will look closely at a number of scholars who view the synagogue as the best analogous model for Pauline church formation.

The second chapter considers the philosophical schools of antiquity. Although the schools were not always physical locations, there were enough philosophical organizations extant in the first century to suggest that Paul's communities would look to them as an organizational model. The chapter opens by examining a few texts which have been understood to indicate that early Pauline Christianity had some contact with philosophical schools. Following a description of how a number of these "schools" constituted themselves, it examines briefly the similarities in propagation between Paul and some philosophers. It then turns to a summary of the works of scholars who understand one or more of the philosophical schools to be the best analogous group for understanding early Pauline communities.

The third chapter is an examination of how the initiation rituals and subsequent community formation affiliated with the ancient mysteries might inform our understanding of Paul's formation of churches. It begins with a summary of some contacts between Paul's letters and the mysteries. After briefly describing the nature and extent of the mysteries in antiquity as well as their propagation, the work of earlier scholars who find similarities between Pauline Christianity and the mysteries is described. Unlike the other models investigated in this book, there is a vast number of negative reactions to the use of the mysteries in understanding Paul's communities. We will survey some representative works from this perspective before turning our attention briefly to more recent uses of the mysteries as an analogy to Pauline church formation.

The fourth chapter begins with a summary of a particularly detailed comparison of a voluntary association at Philadelphia, in Asia Minor, and the Pauline communities. Voluntary associations were formed in antiquity by individuals who gathered together for a shared purpose, often as a result of some common interest. Once we have described in detail some of the purposes and interests of the members of voluntary associations, we briefly suggest some ways in which such groups were propagated. Finally, we examine the work of scholars who have investigated how an understanding of the voluntary associations in antiquity help us to better understand Pauline church formation. In so doing, we give some attention to objections raised to this model and the recent arguments countering these objections.

The concluding chapter briefly discusses the thesis of Jonathan Z. Smith (1990) that, when studying antiquity, the comparison of groups and/or texts can be helpful without necessarily indicating a genealogical connection. It then offers some comments on the implications of the study of Pauline church formation for the contemporary church.

Before turning our attention to the aforementioned models of community formation, we should take a short detour into another institution sometimes referred to as an analogous model for Pauline churches.

Households and House Churches

House Churches in the New Testament

A careful reading of both Acts and Paul's letters quickly reveals that, in a number of cases, the Christian community at a particular location was composed of a "household" or a collection of households.[5] According to Acts, the early church was first formed from a number of smaller cells of Christians, seemingly composed of household units (Acts 2:47; 5:42). Probably they met in a large room within the house, perhaps even an "upstairs room," as is indicated in Acts 1:13 and 20:6–9. This pattern was continued throughout Acts, where we find a number of households converting to Christianity, including that of Cornelius (Acts 10:1–11:18), Lydia (Acts 16:15), the Philippian jailer (Acts 16:31–34), and Crispus (Acts 18:8).

In Paul's letters there are a number of references to the meetings of Christian households, identified by the individuals in whose home they meet: Stephanas (1 Cor 1:16; 16:15), Prisca and Aquila (1 Cor 16:19; Rom 16:3–5), Philemon (Phlm 2), Aristobulus (Rom 16:10), Narcissus (Rom 16:11) and the household of Caesar (Phil 4:22); cf. Nympha (Col 4:15). Along with this there are other, more vague references that most likely indicate Christian house churches (e.g., those named and unnamed in Rom 16:14–15 [Meeks 1983:75] and the factions mentioned in 1 Cor 1:11–12).[6] In light of these striking references to Christian "households," some have proposed that the household is the best analogy for understanding the formation of Paul's communities.

The Nature of Households and House Churches

In antiquity (as also today) institutions might be labeled "public" or "private" (Banks 1994:6; Winter 1994:2). Public institutions traditionally were concerned with the *polis,* the day-to-day business of the city. The private sphere was the *oikos,* or "the household," to which an individual belonged (through birth, slavery or employment). In the Hellenistic age the strict division between the public sphere and the private sphere became increasingly blurred, although one can still speak of institutions as being in one of these two spheres. Paul's churches, as well as each of the analogous groups that we are considering, can be placed in the sphere of the "private." For the most part, they do not have a significant role in the public life of a city, at least during the first century. No group fits this designation of "private" so well as the household, as it was the very basis for private life.

The household was usually an extended household. Under Roman law the oldest male was the head, the *paterfamilias,* and all other members of the household were under his authority, including children, grandchildren, slaves and even employees, if the *paterfamilias* happened to be a landowner or manufacturer (cf. Garnsey and Saller 1987:127).[7] In the absence of a male *paterfamilias* (usually due to death) in certain cases a woman could assume the headship of a household (see Garnsey and Saller 1987:130–36; Horsley 1982:29). If the head of a household converted to a different way of life (a philosophical school or a different religion, including some of the mysteries, Judaism or Christianity) he or she did so with the whole household. All members of the household were to convert without any choice in the matter. In fact, a number of texts of the New Testament indicate that the head of a household converted with the result that an entire household was baptized into the Christian faith (i.e., Stephanus in Corinth [1 Cor 1:16] and Lydia in Philippi [Acts 16:15]). This household would then become the nucleus of the newly formed group, especially if the family involved was wealthy.[8]

The house church can be characterized as a domestic residence which has not been altered structurally and is used, in whole or in part, by the local Christian community for casual assembly (White 1990:104–5; cf. Blue 1994:125). Christians would meet there for any number of reasons, including convenience, for want of another place of worship, in imitation of synagogue worship, because the setting provided facilities necessary for the fellowship (i.e., a kitchen and dining room), or to remain inconspicuous and retain privacy (Blue 1994:121). A number of such house churches have been identified, and some excavated, particularly in recent years.[9] Prior to Constantine's edict of 313 C.E., recognizing Christianity as the religion of the Empire, there were three stages in the development of Christian places of worship (see White 1990:102–39, summarized in Blue 1994:124–30). The first period covers 50–150, when Christians met in private homes belonging to members. In the second period, from 150–250, private residences were renovated for exclusive use by the Christian communities for worship. During the final stage (250–313), larger buildings and halls were constructed.[10]

Households as a Model

One of the first scholars to highlight "The Significance of the Early House Churches" was *Floyd V. Filson,* in 1939. Filson suggested that an understanding of the actual physical conditions under which the early Christians lived and met together would enhance our exegetical understanding of the New Testament texts. Filson pointed out the large amount of evidence for the existence of these house churches that can be found in the New Testament itself, in the writings of the early church fathers, and in the archaeological record (namely, at the church of San Clemente in Rome, Dura Europas in Syria and Priene in Asia Minor). In fact, the archaeological records indicate that small group meetings in private homes eventually grew and developed into larger bodies that needed more space than was available in private dwellings. This necessitated extensions to these dwellings to the point at which they became separately identifiable buildings ("churches").

Filson outlines five ways in which understanding early Christian groups as formed from households into "house churches" can further our understanding of the early church more generally. First, rather than seeing the early Christians being rooted exclusively in the synagogues of Judaism, the house churches help us see how Christians were able to develop their own distinct worship and fellowship. Second, it explains why great attention is paid to family life in the letters of Paul (and others). Third, the existence of more than one house church in a city explains the divisions extant in a particular location. For example, the divisions at Corinth are probably centered around competing house churches. Fourth, we are better able to get a sense of the social status of early Christians. While the majority were undoubtedly poor, some must have attained modest wealth and success, enough that they could own a home in which a larger group could meet. Finally, the fixed church leadership structure can best be understood if seen as developing out of the concept of leadership in the household.

Some twenty years later, *E. A. Judge* published a short study on *The Social Pattern of Christian Groups in the First Century* (1960), in which he investigated the readers of the New Testament texts, who they were and what they thought (1960b:9–10). In order to understand the social precepts of the New Testament, Judge describes the Hellenistic social institutions under which they lived (1960b:16–17). He begins with an examination of the political institutions of the Roman period during the first century. Although the Romans had authoritarian power, they relied heavily on local government. Thus, many cities enjoyed the benefits of the Roman Empire while still holding to some (albeit limited) local autonomy (1960b:23). However, ultimate disillusionment with the benefits of such restricted autonomy led many individuals to seek other means to create mutual beneficial societies (1960b:29).

The first of these "mutual societies" that Judge explores is the household. The household was the place of solidarity in terms of both kinship ties and religious beliefs. Personal loyalty to the household was such that when the head of a house was converted to Christianity (or another religion), all of the members of that same household would be baptized into the new faith (1960b:35–36). Thus, the household became one of the primary building blocks of the Christian faith.

However, Judge moves beyond the household as an adequate model in and of itself. There remained many people in the empire for whom neither political community nor the household was found to be satisfactory (1960b:38). Many such people found solace in one of the associations of individuals which were growing, both in number and in size, in the Roman Empire—the voluntary associations or the philosophical schools. Judge goes on to summarize the affinities that the church had with such associations (we will return to his views below).

Vincent Branick, in his study of *The House Church in the Writings of Paul* (1989), summarizes the New Testament evidence for house churches and the Hellenistic background for understanding the composition and function of the household.[11] He understands the household to be the basis for the early Pauline communities. However, it is merely the means by which Christian community is formed. In terms of structure and organization of the community, Branick suggests that the synagogue provides the "closest parallels" to the Christian community (1989:52).[12]

Conclusion

Clearly, an understanding of ancient households is very helpful for understanding the formation of the earliest Christian groups. However, this model is not mutually exclusive of the other models to be investigated in the following chapters. In fact, there is evidence from each of the other models that, at least in some cases, the groups formed themselves using the household as a base, either by having entire households join or by using fictive kinship language to reflect a new household. For example, we have inscriptional evidence of households which were structured as voluntary associations,[13] and households which were the basis for both synagogues[14] and the mysteries.[15] Private households were also the locus for much philosophical teaching and even some philosophical schools.[16] Since the same is true of Christianity, it seems to be the case that households were often the basic cells of church formation and a vital factor in the church's development (Filson 1939:112; Meeks 1983:75; Stambaugh and Balch 1986:140). However, this does not exclude profitable investigation of other models which built on this foundation.

1
Synagogues

Paul and the Synagogue in Acts

From its origins in Jerusalem the early church grew and expanded throughout the Roman Empire. One of the key players in this expansion began as a persecutor of the church, but was soon converted through a miraculous encounter with the risen Jesus. He went on to take the gospel message to the Gentiles living throughout the empire. Of course, we are talking about Paul, the apostle to the Gentiles. The description thus far we know from both Paul's letters and from the account in Acts.

Acts describes Paul's first stop on his initial missionary journey this way: "When they arrived at Salamis, they proclaimed the word of God in the synagogues of the Jews" (Acts 13:5). On the next stop, at Pisidian Antioch, Paul delivers a word of exhortation to the people in the synagogue there (Acts 13:13–41). Invited back on the next sabbath, Paul and Barnabas were followed by "many Jews and devout converts to Judaism" (Acts 13:43). However, by the next sabbath the Jewish leaders spoke out against the missionaries, prompting them to announce that they would proclaim the message to the Gentiles, who subsequently received the message with joy (Acts 13:44–49). Thus the basic pattern of Paul's missionary strategy is set: Paul and his companions go first to the synagogue where they have some success with both Jews and "God-fearers." They then experience opposition by the Jewish leadership and turn instead to the Gentiles, who more favorably accept their message.

Unfortunately, Paul never describes the logistics of his missionary strategy in detail in his letters. This picture of Paul going first to the synagogue of each city and, for the most part, making his first converts from among those attending the synagogue, is relayed only in the book of Acts. As many first year students of the Bible quickly discover, Acts is a secondary source for Paul's life, and as such must be considered carefully before its evidence is accepted as historically accurate (Knox 1987:3–90). Paul's own letters are the primary source and ought to be given priority. Nevertheless, as we shall see below, many scholars do accept the basic picture given in Acts, and find in the synagogues an adequate analogy for understanding the formation and structure of Paul's churches. However, before turning to a discussion of these scholars we must first outline some of the issues surrounding the nature and extent of the first-century Jewish synagogues.

Nature and Extent of First Century Synagogues

Description

Although there are suggestions in rabbinic literature, Philo and Josephus, and even the New Testament (Acts 15:21) that the synagogue practices go back to the time of Moses, the institution is not likely to have been in evidence in some recognizable form until, at the earliest, the sixth century B.C.E. or, at the latest, the early second century B.C.E. (Burtchaell 1992:202–4; Urman and Flesher 1995:xx–xxiv).

The evidence from the first century C.E. suggests that Jews met in private houses on the Sabbath for meetings focused on personal purity and prayer, and they probably shared a meal together (Kee 1990:8–14). Evidence from the first century also indicates that the word "synagogue" primarily refers to the organized community of Jews who met for worship (a "gathering together"), and not to a particular building wherein they met (Burtchaell 1992:202; cf. Urman and Flesher 1995:xix). Prior to the first century the building was usually referred to as a *proseuchē,* although by the first century, *synagōguē* was applied to both the assembly and the building (Urman and Flesher 1995:xix). However, at what point in the first century *synagōguē* came to be used of the building is the subject of much debate.

Later developments suggest that, in general, the synagogue was governed by a group of elders in a presbyterial form of government (Burtchaell 1992:204). As an organization the synagogue provided a number of services for the Jews living in a particular locale. During the Greco-Roman period the synagogues would undertake any number of civic administrative matters depending upon the level of active government practiced by the imperial authorities. In those places with little government the synagogue could take on "the full apparatus of a civil municipality" (Burtchaell 1992:206). Alongside the religious functions, a local synagogue might also take on such roles as tax collection service, social welfare agency, hospitality center for strangers, archive for important documents and valuables, and community hall. For the Jews "the instrumentality for virtually all communal aspects of life beyond the family—religious, civic, economic and educational—was found in their local synagogues" (Burtchaell 1992:227). Each local assembly was governmentally autonomous, with no greater outside authority. Each saw itself as a "microcosm of the full assembly of Israel" (Burtchaell 1992:215). Nevertheless, there were connections with the Temple in Israel in the form of a "temple tax" sent by each assembly to Jerusalem, although local autonomy and local allegiance remained high (cf. Burtchaell 1992:220).

Unfortunately, evidence for this description of the synagogue comes from later than the first century, primarily from the Talmud and the Mishnah, which is read back into the first century, often without justification. Only one instance of inscriptional evidence can be cited for such diverse functions—the "Theodotus" inscription from Jerusalem (*CIJ* 1404). Although this is often assumed to come from the first century C.E., it now seems more probable that it dates from at least the second century or later.[1]

Howard Clark Kee (1990) has argued that this shift from *proseuchē* to *synagōguē* happened in the late first or early second century. He notes that literary texts reveal that the oldest evidence we have for the use of *synagōguē* for a building comes from the late third century C.E. Until that point *synagōguē* is used to characterize the community that gathers, while *proseuchē* is used to designate the building (1990:6). He also offers the archaeological observation that prior to 200 C.E. there is no evidence that the synagogues in Palestine were architecturally distinguishable edifices (1990:9). Jewish places of worship in the Diaspora from prior to the first century are missing many of the characteristics of third-century C.E. synagogues and in fact each seems to have been understood as a *proseuchē*. Studies of the Pharisees in the first century give no indication of a formal pattern of worship or organization. All of this evidence suggests that Jews prior to the end of the first century were involved in "informal gatherings for fresh appropriation of the Torah, for the strengthening of group identity, and for heightening devotion to the God of Israel" (1990:14). Thus, when Luke refers to Paul and his associates entering synagogues to preach and teach, he is reflecting a later (post-70 C.E.) form of synagogal worship back onto the time of the early church (1990:18).

As with any conclusion drawn on the basis of archaeological and literary evidence, Kee's conclusion has not gone unchallenged. ***Richard E. Oster*** (1993) has come to Luke's defense in suggesting that Kee has misrepresented some of the evidence by focusing too narrowly on the use of the words *proseuchē* and *synagōguē,* overlooking important literary evidence such as is found in Josephus, and misreading the archaeological data. Oster concludes that Luke's picture of the Jewish synagogues is not anachronistic, and actually fits well with what is known of synagogues in the pre-70 period. Kee's short rejoinder (1994) attempts to discredit some of Oster's claims, as does his later article on the Theodotus inscription (1995). It is clear that the debate is not likely to subside in the near future, and how one settles the question will affect, among other things, how one understands the early formation of Pauline communities.

Jewish Proselytism

It has always been a fairly certain assumption on the part of scholars that in the first century Jews, particularly Pharisees, sought converts to Judaism through aggressive missionary practices (see summary in McKnight 1991:1–4). The appeal of Judaism for the Gentiles was its monotheism, national privilege and emphasis on morality, all of which were used by the Jewish missionaries to attract converts. This missionary impulse is seen to be confirmed in Matthew when Jesus condemns the "scribes and the Pharisees" because they "cross sea and land to make a single convert (*proselyton*)" (Matt 23:15). This missionary zeal, it is suggested, was the prototype for the Christian missionaries, who likewise went into the world to make converts, first to their own branch of Judaism and ultimately, to their new religion. Thus, Paul is seen as doing much the same as a Christian as he did as a Pharisee, but for a different cause.

Recent studies have called this assumption into question. *Scot McKnight,* in his *A Light Among the Gentiles* (1991), argues that although the ancient texts indicate that there were Gentile converts to Judaism, "Second Temple Judaism was largely unconcerned with missionary activity" and "was not a missionary religion" (McKnight 1991:7). McKnight surveys a number of ways in which Jews were integrated into their Hellenistic environment, and at the same time were antagonistic toward it. So, while Hellenistic education, friendliness toward Gentiles and assimilation of some ideas led to an openness on the part of the Jews, the conviction of being God's chosen people and the covenant of Abraham and Moses caused the Jewish people to guard themselves from contamination by setting up social boundaries which kept Gentiles at a distance. In sum, the Jewish people were both "holy and kind" with regard to the Gentiles (McKnight 1991:29).

McKnight's second and third chapters are the most crucial, as here he reexamines ancient material which discusses converts to Judaism. This material shows that although "Jews were generally favorably disposed to Gentiles who were willing to convert to Judaism" (1991:45), "there is almost no evidence that Jews were involved in evangelizing Gentiles and aggressively drawing Gentiles into their religion" (1991:48). Most of the means whereby Gentiles converted to Judaism involved "passive" evangelism. God's mighty deeds might convince some, while others might be exposed to Jewish literature aimed at establishing Jewish identity and thus be converted. Certainly synagogues were open for Gentiles to come in and be taught, and the education of abandoned Gentile babies by Jews led to their being considered "Jewish." Most effective was the living of a good life and the doing of good deeds which would serve to attract others to Judaism. In this regard, the Jewish attitude toward outsiders was to be "a light among the Gentiles" (1991:48). What is clearly lacking from the ancient testimony is evidence of anything but a few evangelists who actively sought to convert Gentiles (1991:75). "In short, it can be said that Judaism was not a missionary religion" (1991:77).

Two studies published by **Martin Goodman** (*Mission and Conversion* [1994] and "Jewish Proselytizing in the First Century" [1992] 53–78) concur with McKnight's conclusions. His own reexamination of the evidence put forth to suggest that first-century Jews pursued an active mission to win proselytes concludes that such a position is "very weak" and, in fact, that there is good reason to deny the existence of such a mission (1992:70). Although there is some evidence of a Jewish mission to win Gentile sympathizers to Judaism, it "is a far cry from the universal proselytizing mission" that is often assumed for the first century (1994:87–88). Although Gentiles would not be denied access to Judaism, most Jews saw their role as passively bearing witness to their faith; "how the Gentiles reacted to such a witness was up to them" (1992:72).

What is most significant from the studies of McKnight and Goodman for our purpose is the evidence amassed against what in the past has always been thought to be the case: that the synagogues of the first century were the base of an aggressive Jewish mission to convert Gentiles (see Jeremias 1958:11–19; Georgi 1986:83–151, esp. 84). The synagogue-based "Jewish mission" can no longer be seen as the prototype of the Christian missionary impulse because it simply did not exist. What we find instead is that the evidence suggests a more passive role for the synagogue in accepting its few converts along with a large number of Jewish sympathizers, often called "God-fearers," without actively pursuing them.[2] It is to this latter group that we now turn as, once again, recent scholarly inquiry has made it a controversial topic.

The Existence of God-Fearers

At a number of points in his narrative, Luke suggests that early Christian groups were formed from a group attached to the synagogue and described in Acts as "those who fear God" (*hoi phoboumenoi ton theon,* Acts 10:2, 22, 35; 13:16, 26) and "those who revere God" (*hoi sebomenoi ton theon,* Acts 13:43, 50; 16:14; 17:4, 17; 18:7). The phrases do not seem to be used of Jews, but indicate Gentile sympathizers who were attracted to the Jewish religion and had a close relationship with the synagogue, even attending meetings. However, it is unlikely that people designated as such had fully converted to Judaism, thus becoming proselytes (*prosēlytos;* Lüdemann 1987:155; Acts 2:10; 6:5; 13:43; cf. Matt 23:15). Such a group of "sympathizers," often designated by the technical term "God-fearers," has long been assumed to exist and is often used to explain the origins of Pauline groups from the early synagogues; Paul evangelized in the synagogues with the result of converting Gentile God-fearers, thus becoming the "apostle to the Gentiles." However, of late, the very existence of this group has been called into question.

A. T. Kraabel[3] has argued strongly against the existence of a large group of "God-fearers" who attached themselves to the synagogues of Diaspora Judaism. In his 1981 article, "The Disappearance of the God-Fearers," he notes that it is the book of Acts which provided the initial description to which other evidence was adapted: "Always the *technical terms* were drawn from Luke....These are *phoboumenos* and *sebomenos,* which appear in Acts, and *theosebēs,* which was thought to be a variant of the latter term," and appears frequently in the inscriptions (Kraabel 1981:114–15, his emphasis). He thinks it unlikely that Luke is to be trusted as a reliable source attesting to the existence of such a group, especially when they fit into his presentation so well.[4]

Kraabel examines six Diaspora synagogue sites, and finds that there is no evidence of Gentile adhesion to Judaism in these cities (Dura Europas, Sardis, Priene, Delos, Stobi and Ostia). While this "argument from silence" (Hemer 1983:54) cannot prove conclusively that there never was a large circle of God-fearers associated with Diaspora synagogues, it does call Luke's presentation into question. Kraabel points out that "the new evidence required to falsify this hypothesis would have to be substantial; one clear inscription using the term *phoboumenos* or *sebomenos* precisely as in Acts would be helpful, but not sufficient, since at most it might prove God-fearers for that particular synagogue community" (1981:121).

One such inscription might be the inscription from the synagogue at Aphrodisias (early third century C.E. [ca. 210]; Reynolds and Tannenbaum 1987:5–7) which many have taken to indicate the existence of God-fearers. The use of *theosebēs* ("God-fearer") in the Aphrodisias inscription is described and discussed briefly by Tannenbaum

(1986:56–57). He focuses on the predominance of the *theosebeis* in the inscription and the similarity it evokes to people mentioned in the Talmud and the early church writings, concluding that those designated as such in the inscription were attracted to the synagogue but had not yet become full converts.

The use of this inscription is problematic. First, this particular evidence is quite late for understanding Pauline Christianity. Second, the term used is *theosebēs* (l. 34), which is not used in Acts. Third, as Tannenbaum himself points out (1986:57), the mention in the inscription of nine members of the city council who would have been required to sacrifice to one or more pagan gods shows that "God-fearers" were able to attach themselves to a synagogue without relinquishing the worship of other deities. Murphy-O'Connor (1992:122) points out that Tannenbaum does not take seriously the indications in the inscription that it was placed at the entrance to a soup kitchen. Such a building "met a social need to which it would have been perfectly natural for Gentiles with a sense of civic duty to subscribe because it benefited the city and not merely the Jewish community." The title *theosebēs* here is simply a compliment to the moral character of the pagan donors. Thus, one should not assume *theosebēs* had a technical or quasi-technical sense in antiquity. In fact, the term may indicate nothing more than that Gentiles were friendly to Jews as fellow townspeople (MacLennan and Kraabel 1986:51).[5]

Evidence that the designation "worshiper of God" is a Lukan construct is based upon Luke's predilection for designating as such Gentiles who turn to Christianity. Other Gentiles designated as "Jewish sympathizers" in Luke-Acts include a centurion (Luke 7:5),[6] an Ethiopian eunuch (Acts 8:27–28), and Cornelius (Acts 10:2; cf. his attendant, 10:7). The "God-fearers" seem to be used in order not to disrupt Luke's pattern of presenting Paul as approaching first the Jews and then the Gentiles (cf. Kraabel 1994:85). Thus, Kraabel concludes,

> The God-fearers are on the stage as needed, off the stage after they have served their purpose in the plot. Acts cannot be used as evidence that there ever were such groups in the synagogues of the Roman Empire. (Kraabel 1981:121; Kraabel 1994:85)

He then suggests that "The God-fearers are a symbol to help Luke show how Christianity had become a Gentile religion *legitimately* and without losing its Old Testament roots" (Kraabel 1981:121, his emphasis).

Not everyone has readily accepted Kraabel's work.[7] For example, despite disagreeing with Tannenbaum's understanding of the nine donors to the soup kitchen mentioned in the Aphrodisias inscription, *Jerome Murphy-O'Connor* ("Lots of God-fearers? *Theosebeis* in the Aphrodisias Inscription" [1992] 423–24) suggests that the two men named earlier in the inscription as *theosebeis* are, in fact, part of the Jewish community, although they have not yet reached a stage where they might be called proselytes. This is confirmed by a Jewish manumission inscription from the first century C.E. (CIRB 71). These inscriptions show that the designation *theosebēs* did exist and is not simply a theological construct of Luke. However, Murphy-O'Connor cautions that the term is ambiguous and can be used in different senses depending on the context; a single definition should not simply be assumed.

J. Andrew Overman, "The God-Fearers: Some Neglected Features" (1992), is much more critical of Kraabel's work, pointing out that he has overlooked significant evidence for the existence of "a class, or group of gentiles who were involved in or attracted to the life of the Jewish community in the Roman Diaspora" (1992:146). Overman shows how various expressions in the LXX suggest that there has long existed a class of non-Jewish people attracted to Judaism who eventually came to be known as "God-fearers," and Luke would have been aware of this. Overman goes on to show that while the exact expression which occurs in Acts, *hoi phoboumenoi/sebomenoi ton theon,* may not occur in literature and inscriptions from the period, other descriptions in writers such as Josephus, Philo and Juvenal (*Satire* 14, c.130) and inscriptions from Acmonea and Sardis suggest that such a group existed. In fact, Overman concludes that "Gentiles were apparently drawn to Judaism in significant numbers" (1992:151).

We see from these writers that Kraabel is perhaps too strong in his denial of the existence of Gentiles sympathetic to Judaism in the first century. The attraction of eastern cults throughout the empire would certainly have brought some inquisitors to Judaism. However, his caution about accepting too readily the presentation in Acts is well-founded and should cause all scholars to be cautious in their use of Luke's picture of the formation of early Pauline churches. The problem in much of the literature is not so much the existence of Gentiles attracted to Judaism, but the size of this group. The sketchy amount of evidence suggests that one should not be too quick to posit a large number of "God-fearers" without more substantial evidence.

Synagogues as a Model

The controversy that surrounds the nature of the first-century synagogues, the existence of a Jewish mission and the presence of a category of "God-fearers" attached to the synagogues continues unabated. However, within these debates a number of scholars have found evidence that the synagogue is the best analogy for understanding the formation and structure of the early Pauline churches, primarily because these churches were a direct development out of the synagogues.

According to *John G. Gager, Kingdom and Community* (1975: 126–29; 135–40),[8] Diaspora Judaism provided the "blueprint" for Christianity when it was adapting to the Greco-Roman world outside of Palestine in a number of ways: the use of sacred scripture (the LXX), methods of interpretation, recensions of Jewish documents (e.g., Sibylline Oracles), the influence of Philo and the provision of a place for Christian missionaries to attempt to win converts—the synagogue. The Christian communities adopted the basic structure of the Diaspora synagogues for their meetings in terms of leadership, liturgical practices and social practice. Christianity triumphed over Judaism in socio-political terms because Diaspora Judaism never reached its potential as a "major universal religion" (1975:139), and Hellenistic Christianity offered all of the advantages of the Jewish religion without the obligations of the ritual law or the connections with a national identity (1975:139–40).[9]

In his 1985 article "Breaking Away: Three New Testament Pictures of Christianity's Separation from the Jewish Communities" (1985), *Wayne A. Meeks* argues that in any given urban center there was little contact between the Pauline Christian groups and the Jewish communities. Arguing from Paul's letters rather than the picture in Acts, he suggests that the form of organization for Pauline Christian groups was the household, not the synagogue, and, apart from some conflict between Paul and the Jews, there was very little conflict between the two groups. Although theologically Judaism played a central part in the identity of Pauline Christianity, socially the Pauline groups were not a sect of Judaism but "organized their lives independently from the Jewish associations of the cities where they were founded, and apparently, so far as the evidence reveals, they had little or no interaction with the Jews" (1985:106).

While Meeks is quite right to suggest that Pauline Christian identity was not formed from once being within the Jewish context, his pointing to the household is not a viable alternative. As we saw in the introduction, the household was the basis of most small group formation in antiquity, including synagogues. Thus, Meeks needs to be more specific in finding an analogy. In fact, in a slightly earlier work (1983), he is. In briefly describing the various models available for understanding early Christian group formation, Meeks (1983:80–81) calls the Jewish synagogue "the nearest and most natural model" for understanding the urban Christian groups, as these groups were an offshoot of Judaism (1983:80; cf. 1986:110).[10] There are a number of similarities. First, both Jewish and Christian groups had a sense of belonging to a larger movement beyond the local group. Second, Paul's use of *ekklēsia* is similar to the special usage of the word by Greek-speaking Jews (although Meeks can cite no evidence that it was used of a synagogue). Third, both groups used private dwellings for meetings, and the structures of the meetings were "probably" similar.

Meeks also has to admit to a number of differences. Terminology for officers seems to be different, women are accorded a greater role,[11] the membership requirements of the churches are broader than ethnic background and Paul rejects certain Jewish rituals (e.g., circumcision). Thus, while the synagogue is, for Meeks, the best model, it is still deficient in fully explaining the phenomenon of the formation of Paul's churches.[12]

James Burtchaell's 1992 study, *From Synagogue to Church,* focuses on ecclesial offices in the early church. He traces the history of the discussion from the Reformation to the modern period. He maps the development of the argument for the origins of the ecclesial offices in the New Testament itself (that is, in the earliest communities) and the contrary point that church offices began later, in the second century.

According to Burtchaell, the "consensus view" has gone virtually unchallenged over six centuries: the early church was unorganized and spontaneous, with no authority figures or offices. As a consequence, this became the ideal for the modern church which wanted to base itself on the New Testament ideal. As a result of this study, in the second half of the book he argues against many modern interpretations by suggesting that from its very beginning, the church had officials who presided at the liturgy. However, these people did not have the upmost authority in the community; this belonged to the charismatic lay people who were inspired of God to make pronouncements (as reflected in both the New Testament and other early Christian writings such as the *Didache*).

The second half of the book is more significant for our investigation. Burtchaell examines the evidence from the ancient Jewish communities and shows how the Christian churches actually continued the offices of the synagogue. After sketching the history of the synagogue and describing briefly the various functions which it had within the Jewish community (in Palestine and the Diaspora), Burtchaell turns his attention to his central concern—the officers of the synagogue (1992:228–63). He concludes that within the vast array of evidence there is a tradition of community programs, services and offices that could be characterized as typical of the Jewish synagogues. This is important as he turns to the Christian churches to investigate whether an analogous pattern can be discerned that would show the continuation from synagogue to church.

Methodologically, Burtchaell wants to allow for "shifts in nomenclature" and "distinctively Christian developments" when explaining how the structure of Christian groups arose from the synagogue model (1992:274). This methodological caveat, however, quickly becomes the weak link in his argument. Burtchaell argues for the direct continuity from synagogue to church, but almost immediately, with regard to nomenclature for the groups (i.e., Paul's use of *ekklēsia* and never *synagōguē*) and the group officials, he has to allow that "the Christians were beginning to differentiate themselves" from the Jewish communities (1992:278). He attempts to diminish this problem by suggesting that "nomenclature is not structure" (1992:278), but has not proved this. In fact, Burtchaell seems to assume what he seeks to prove throughout his investigation. That is, he assumes that there was continuity from synagogue to church and then seeks to explain all of the differences as the

Christians breaking away from the Jewish groups. However, he never presents a compelling argument for the continuity he assumes. The differences that he notes in membership, leadership, property ownership and nomenclature (summarized 1992:340–48) seem to vastly outweigh the similarities in function that he describes (1992:339–40). In fact, some of the functions (prayer, ritual meals, discussion of community policy, enforcement of discipline, choosing of officers, burial of the dead and maintenance of cemeteries) are general enough to be true of many types of groups, with no obvious link required between churches and synagogues. The similarity in worldwide organization, wherein there are no locally autonomous communities, simply misreads the evidence (see Ascough 1997). Compounding these problems is Burtchaell's blending of Palestinian Christianity with Christian groups elsewhere (i.e., Pauline groups in urban areas; cf. 1992:336, 352),[13] and thus his failure to recognize fundamental differences among the Christian groups themselves.

Michael D. Goulder ("Silas in Thessalonica," 1992) has suggested that the church was born "from the womb of the synagogue." His work is summarized in ***Judith M. Lieu*** ("Do God-fearers Make Good Christians?" 1994), who takes as her starting point that the church was originally formed from within the synagogue and, as such, attracted to itself a number of God-fearers. These God-fearers had a sympathy for monotheism and a high regard for the ethical judgments it required. Not only this, they were also very familiar with the revelation of God in the history and experience of the Jewish people, as recorded in the texts of the LXX. Thus, Paul is able to argue in his letters by appeals to Scripture in a way that presupposes a certain familiarity with these texts (1994:333).

These God-fearers were prevented from becoming full members of the synagogue because it required circumcision, a "morally abhorrent as well as painful if not life-threatening" procedure (1994:334).[14] However, Christianity affirmed the ethical monotheism of Judaism while also offering these God-fearers full membership in the community. Thus, many of them became Christians, and their commitment to monotheism and a high ethical standard would have made them "good" Christians. Lieu contrasts them to pagans, whom she suggests would not have had a "full understanding" of Christianity and would have carried over remnants of their "old ways," presumably making them "bad" Christians. This fringe adherence to Judaism is also the primary weakness for those God-fearers who become Christians. Their desire for obedience to the law (e.g., food requirements, calendar observance and circumcision) would have been unfulfilled within Christianity and would have made them easy victims for the Jewish-Christian mission (1994:335).

Lieu's reconstruction is informative about the crossover between Judaism and Christianity and back. Unfortunately, however, those who accept this picture simply assume too quickly the presence of God-fearers behind some texts of Paul and do not pay adequate attention to other Pauline texts. All too often we find Paul addressing situations in which "pagan" converts have regressed to old patterns of living, and, by their logic, could not therefore have been God-fearers (e.g., the many moral dilemmas facing the Corinthians). More significantly, this reconstruction assumes a pattern of "quick conversion" as it is demonstrated in Acts. The understanding of God's interaction with God's people and a subsequent commitment to ethical monotheism could have been reached gradually under Paul's tutelage. This is especially so in areas where there does not seem to have been a strong Jewish presence in the first century (e.g., Philippi and Thessalonica).

In fact, Lieu herself recognizes the problem with the reconstruction. She suggests that the "'attachment to the synagogue' has to be interpreted not in terms of personal religious needs and commitment but in a wider framework of social allegiance and status" (1994:337). That is to say, God-fearers did not simply have pious motivations; a number of social factors made it desirable to them to be involved in the network of relationships the Jewish community established. Social and political advantage could be gained by supporting the synagogue and is probably behind the two well-known examples of God-fearers, the Gentile patron Julia Severa of Acmonia (*CIJ* 766) and the nine civic councilors who donate to the Jewish charitable organization at Aphrodisias.

Lieu concludes that while there would have been some Gentiles who were attracted to Judaism for religious reasons, many others were attracted for the social advantages it offered. However, it is not self-evident that they subsequently became good Christians, or even became Christians at all, since Christianity, at least in its early stages, did not offer the social advantages that Judaism did. Decisions to become an adherent of Judaism or Christianity were not limited to theological arguments but involved a complex of social issues (1994:345).

In his *Who Are the People of God?* (1995), **Howard Clark Kee** attempts to produce a set of models for early Christian community in which each of the various Christian groups can be placed. However, each of his five models come from Judaism: the community of the wise, the Law-abiding community, the community where God dwells among his people, the community of mystical participation and the ethnically and culturally inclusive community. Each is illustrated from Jewish texts. Kee argues that each of these models was adapted by one or more of the Christian groups until the Christian groups themselves evolved into a more formal structure and organization.

Paul's communities fit into the paradigm as "communities of the wise."[15] Such a community sees itself as having been elected by God to receive a special wisdom. By studying this wisdom, life could be lived in a world of uncertainty. This issue is often addressed through apocalyptic literature. In Judaism this includes Ben Sira, Wisdom of Solomon, Daniel, 1 and 2 Enoch, Jubilees, 2 Baruch and 4 Ezra. Kee suggests that the writings of early Christian communities that reflect this tradition are the Sayings Source (Q),[16] Paul's letters, Revelation, Jude and 2 Peter.

Paul adopts the paradigm of the "community of the wise" because of two powerful influences in his background—his training as a Pharisee and his exposure to the philosophy of Stoicism and Middle Platonism (1995b:73). Paul's Pharisaic training insured his concern with making the scriptures relevant to daily living. The Stoic influence is seen in Paul's concept of the accessibility of natural law and the human capacity to grasp it, moral responsibility and human virtue, and a belief in life after death. Although Kee does allow that Paul may have encountered Stoic philosophy directly in his home town of Tarsus, he thinks it more likely that it was first filtered through Diaspora Judaism. This is particularly so since Judaism had been greatly influenced by the surrounding Greco-Roman culture (1995b:73, cf. 145–57). Thus while philosophical thought is an important background for understanding Paul, Kee assumes that the communities which he founded were very much grounded in Jewish ways of thinking and living. To put it in terms of our own paradigm, they were more like "synagogues" than "philosophical schools."[17]

In his 1995 article "The Early Church: Internal Jewish Migration or New Religion," *Dieter Georgi* argues that all of the evidence from early Christian texts points to Christianity as emerging as one faction of first-century Judaism rather than as a separate religion diametrically opposed to it. Georgi first surveys the early Christian literature to show that in the sphere of life of the early Christians the "Easter experiences" were interpreted in light of Jewish biblical concepts and thus were not seen as antithetical to Judaism. This is true for Jesus and Stephen and even for Paul. Paul's polemic against Jews and things Jewish must be seen in the light of the broader perspective of a history of conflicts and antitheses within the Jewish tradition (1995:46). These antitheses Georgi amply illustrates, drawing on material from sources such as the Old Testament prophets, Josephus, Qumran and the rabbis.

All the evidence points to a number of diverse groups within Judaism which were often antagonistic toward other Jewish groups in the first century. He even suggests that the polemic of one group against another often makes "the New Testament polemic against the Jews appear mild" (1995:46). Since Judaism of the first century was "a colorful, pluralistic phenomenon," the addition of groups of followers of Jesus "could not have made that much of a difference" (1995:48). It was only toward the end of the first century that a few dominant groups began to vie with one another for legitimation in the eyes of the Roman authorities and became mainstream Judaism and mainstream Christianity (1995:65–66).

The tendency towards a multiplicity of groups in the first century Georgi calls "interior migrations within Judaism" (1995:56). It is as such an "interior migration" that the founding of churches by Paul must be understood. Georgi reexamines some of the crucial points at which Paul seems to come into conflict with Judaism. Paul's understanding of the Law (that it "opens up a communal future in which mutual trust is realized," 1995:62) and his understanding of unlimited divine grace had both been explored before within Judaism. While Paul was not simply replicating the concepts of other Jewish groups, neither was he taking previously unheard of steps "into a novel genre of experience, thought, and speech" (1995:63). Paul, then, was a Jewish reformer, not an advocate of a new religion.

Georgi's argument for the multifaceted nature of first-century Judaism is compelling. No doubt many Jewish Christians were, in fact, part of a larger tendency of "migration" within Judaism. However, two issues arise. The first is the question of self-identity of a group. While Matthew's community, and even their predecessors, may have understood themselves to be "on the conservative side of Judaism" (1995:53), they would have considered other groups (more specifically, the radical rabbis) to have abandoned their Jewish heritage. That is to say, for those involved in the disputes, at issue was not migration within a larger category of "Judaism," but "inside/outside" language concerning who were the legitimate heirs of the promises to Israel. The overarching understanding of Jewish migration is more helpful for modern scholars and especially those involved in Christian-Jewish dialogue,[18] but it tells us less about the self-understanding of the groups embroiled in the controversy.

The second issue is related to the first but pertains particularly to Paul. Many of those who came to embrace the "Easter experiences" as conveyed by Paul were not themselves Jewish. Undoubtedly some were, but in many cases not even a majority of a particular community were Jewish (i.e., Galatia, Philippi, Thessalonica). In these cases it is unlikely that in working out a self-identity they would have seen themselves in competition with Jewish groups, but rather with any other groups in general. Thus, Paul's use of *ekklēsia* becomes more significant than Georgi allows. Georgi points out that Paul himself never uses the terms "Christian" or "Christianity," suggesting that he did not know these terms (1995:40). However, as Georgi admits, neither does Paul use *synagōguē* or *proseuchē*. Georgi suggests that he uses *ekklēsia* to deliberately compete with the "assembly of free citizens meeting in the local theater" rather than to compete with local Jewish groups (1995:41). In so doing, however, Paul's groups would also be competing with other small, non-Jewish associations ("voluntary associations") which often took their nomenclature from the civic institutions (and more often not in direct competition but in the sense of "imitation as flattery").

Georgi's article is helpful as a means of locating early Christian-Jewish dialogue in a much larger frame of reference than has previously been allowed, but it is less helpful for understanding the way Pauline communities were formed and the way their self-identity was developed.

Conclusion

With so much of our understanding of the Jewish synagogues being challenged, nuanced and developed with the publication of further literary and archaeological studies, the use of the synagogues as an analogy for early Pauline communities becomes problematic. It is difficult to conclude that Christianity gained its missionary impulse directly from the missionary impulse of Judaism or even to accept at face value the picture in Acts of Paul making his first converts from the synagogues. Nevertheless, there is obviously evidence that Pauline Christianity had much to do with Judaism of the first century, and much can be learned from studying it. However, as we have seen, using the synagogues as an analogy is not without its problems. For this reason other models have been explored by scholars, and it is to these that we now turn.

2
Philosophical Schools

Paul and the Moral Philosophers

Although the predominant picture of Paul's preaching in Acts places Paul in the synagogues of the Jews, there are a couple of instances where Paul is situated among philosophers. According to Acts 17:16–34, when Paul reached Athens he met some Epicurean and Stoic philosophers and was invited to the Areopagus to present his "new teaching" to them. The writer of Acts characterizes the Athenians, and the foreigners living there, as doing nothing but engaging in conversation about new ideas (17:21). The Areopagus was probably the Roman-sanctioned governing body of Athenian citizens (see Gill 1994:447) but clearly, for the writer of Acts, Paul's audience includes among them the Stoic and Epicurean philosophers.

Sometime later, when Paul reached Ephesus, the writer of Acts has him leave the synagogue to preach in the "lecture hall" (*scholē*) of Tyrannus (Acts 19:9). Although the exact meaning of *scholē* is unclear, most associate it with a place or a group of people wherein philosophical discourse could take place.[1] Although the picture in Acts is far from depicting Paul as a Hellenistic moral philosopher, it is not out of keeping with some of Paul's letters. Many scholars have seen in Paul's language in his letters an awareness to use and adapt the popular moral philosophical discourse of his day.

The use of the philosophical schools as an analogy for understanding early Christian groups is not new. Even in antiquity, claims were made for secular philosophers such as Seneca being Christian because of the affinities between his teaching and that of Christianity (see Malherbe 1989c:67–68). More recently, however, attention to the philosophic background of Paul's teachings and practices has been growing. While we cannot enter into the nuances of each philosophical system, nor examine each instance where Paul might be drawing on the language, ideas or strategies of the philosophers, we will highlight those areas where Paul's words may indicate that he constituted his churches along the lines of a philosophical school.

Paul's use of the techniques of the Hellenistic moral philosophers is brought to the fore by the work of *Abraham J. Malherbe,* who has focused on the similarities between Paul's letters (particularly 1 Thessalonians) and the "popular" philosophers of Paul's day such as the Cynics, Stoics and Epicureans.[2] Malherbe's *The Social Aspects of Early Christianity* (1983) is a collection of lectures delivered at Rice University in 1975. These lectures were first published in 1977 and subsequently in revised form (with the addition of an extra chapter and an epilogue) in 1983. In these lectures Malherbe was one of the first of the modern generation of scholars to take seriously the social historical study of early Christianity.[3]

In examining 1 Thessalonians, Malherbe suggests that in the first three chapters Paul uses paraenetic exhortation and the antithetic style, both of which are common in the writings of the moral philosophers of the first century (1983:23). Within this, Paul's references to his working to support himself and his concern for the souls of the Thessalonians (1 Thess 2:9; 4:9–12) shows that he views his ministry among the Thessalonians in much the same way that the philosophers conceived of their own task. The Thessalonians themselves might have organized their community like those of the Epicureans, taking on a air of quietism and withdrawal from society. In this context, Paul's exhortation in 4:9–12 shows that Paul himself disagrees with this strategy and urges the Thessalonians to take seriously what society thinks of them and to have society think well of them by working diligently to support themselves.[4]

In his 1987 study, *Paul and the Thessalonians,* Malherbe attempts to further illuminate Paul's missionary "strategy" in Thessalonica by comparing it to that of the moral philosophers. Both Paul and the moral philosophers used their semiprivate workshop as a forum in which philosophical discourse could take place and a community could be formed (1987:33). Like the moral philosophers, Paul offers himself as the ideal model to be imitated (1 Thess 1:6; Malherbe 1987:52–60) in the shaping of the community. Finally, Paul nurtured his community, both while living among them and in his absence, much like the philosophers nurtured their students (1987:61–94; 1989b:35–48; 67–77). These comparisons do not make Paul a moral philosopher (1987:108), but illuminate his practice and show it to be very much like that of the moral philosophers. Malherbe does not distinguish what type of ancient community might provide the best analogy to the Thessalonian church, but it is clear that a community formed, shaped and nurtured along the same lines as a philosophical school will be most like that particular type of ancient grouping.

Malherbe laments the fact that only those philosophers who provide obvious points of comparison with the New Testament have been studied—Stoic moralists (Seneca, Musonius Rufus, Epictetus, Dio Chrysostom), Plutarch and Lucian (Malherbe 1989a:16; 1992:330). He calls for a much broader investigation of the philosophical schools of antiquity. While some have followed this call, much more work needs to be done.[5]

Like others before him, Malherbe finds the most obvious point of contact between Paul and the popular philosophers in the realm of ethics (1983:48). The lists of virtues and vices and moral commonplaces that are found in the popular moralists are also found in the writings of Paul (and other New Testament books; see Malherbe 1992:278–330). However, he notes that there is a shift occurring in the use of the moral philosophers in understanding the world of the New Testament; "interest has shifted from ethics to ethos" (1992:330). Having listed the works of Judge (1960a), Hock (1980), Stowers (1984) and his own books (1983; 1989), he goes on to suggest that there has yet to be "a full appreciation of the long stride that has been taken from the individualism of Greek ethics to the communal concerns of the early Christians" (1992:330). In what follows we will investigate how some scholars have begun to investigate these communal concerns in light of the philosophical schools.

Nature and Extent of Philosophical Schools

Description

It is clear that "philosophical schools held a dominant place in the Greco-Roman world" (Wilken 1971:272). As with Hellenistic philosophy generally, these schools were concerned as much with how one lives an ethical life as with "ideas." The focus of much of the discussion was on becoming good, with an ultimate goal of human *eudaimonia*, variously translated as "happiness," or "pleasure," or "human flourishing." Through various means such as street corner preaching, formal lectures, letters, essays, treatises, meditations and the like, philosophers conveyed their own understanding of the goal (*telos*) of human life and how to achieve it. In fact, Christianity itself was a "philosophy" insofar as it was concerned to convey a way of leading a virtuous life (Wilken 1984:79). At stake in our discussion is whether or not groups of Christians, particularly those formed by Paul, were organized like the Hellenistic philosophical schools.[6]

The philosophical "schools" were not always physical locations and should not be read to be equivalent to what moderns mean by "church"—that is, a building. The "school" might simply indicate a number of people committed to the same way of life or to following a particular founder. However, some of the philosophical "schools" did form communities of like-minded women and men. "The various schools provided the worldview and practical guidance for life that religion does for many today" (Ferguson 1987:255).

One of the earliest schools was that of Plato in Athens. Plato organized a group of pupils into an association which worshipped the Muses. This association, and the building in which they met, came to be known as the Academy. Other philosophical schools included Aristotle's Lyceum, the Stoics' Poikile and the Epicurean Garden, all located in Athens.

By the time of the first century, only two philosophical groups seem to have formed themselves into a closed organization of initiated disciples—the Pythagoreans and the Epicureans (Meeks 1983:83; Goodman 1994:34). Pythagoras founded a school of philosophy at Croton, southern Italy, which was characterized by a common store of goods, diet and clothing restrictions, and a daily regimen (Meeks

1983:83). The Epicureans, formed into a "school" in the Garden at Athens during the fourth century B.C.E., "talked about themselves as members of a defined community, preserving the ideal of philosophical fraternities which could ensure the orthodoxy of their scattered brothers by oaths to Epicurus, worship his image and [write] epistles to one another to uphold the consistency of the faith" (Goodman 1994:34).

Other philosophies seem not to have become "schools" in the sense of well-defined, physically located groups like the Neopythagorians or the Epicureans. However, there did exist many "schools of thought," and the individual practitioner of a certain philosophical system could be easily identified by his or her particular dress (as was the case with the Cynics) or the style or content of the message proclaimed. He or she would often gather students together in a particular location, thus forming a "school." A philosophical teacher might even gather the students in a public place such as a market, gymnasium or stoa, thus opening up their teachings to the wider public (Stowers 1988:81). It is within this larger framework that Paul and his communities have been understood.

The moral world of the early Christian communities is described well by **Wayne A. Meeks** (*The Moral World of the First Christians,* 1986), who seeks to provide a context in which to understand Christian community formation. He investigates how different groups understood themselves, their world and their relationship to their world. In doing so, he attempts to overcome the principal problem faced by the historian— the lack of evidence for all but a wealthy minority of the people (Meeks 1986:35). The contexts within which individual choices were made were still the traditional roles of individuals in society. Thus, one's sense of what was fair, what was expected, what was honorable depended upon one's place in the social pyramid.

Meeks' focus is the "great traditions" of Greece and Rome. He investigates the "growing individualism" of late Hellenistic ethics as well as the "cosmopolitanism" of some of the philosophical schools. The "schools" were often little more than a lecturer and his pupils who were concerned with the moral formation of the soul ("ethics"). Meeks looks at a number of examples as illustrative of the various schools, including Plutarch (a first- or early-second-century C.E. representative of Middle Platonism), Musonius Rufus (mid-to-late-first-century C.E.

Stoic), the Cynics and the Epicureans. Common to all these "schools" is the thought that the aim of philosophy is the well-wrought life. Ethics is the craft of right living and has to be learned. The rational life, and thus the happy life, is a life lived in accord with nature, where emotion is mistrusted (Meeks 1986:60).

Meeks then turns to the "great traditions" of Israel by looking at a few representative voices: Wisdom of Sirach, Qumran, Philo and the Mishna. Common within all of these was the notion that history teaches morals, that Israel remains God's people (distinctive and separate from those around them), that scripture forms a constitutive role in Jewish ethical discourse and that the law is important. There were two "views" of the law in the sources: on the one hand, the Torah comprises the meaningful structure of the universe (all that is real: Ben Sira, Philo) while on the other, the specific commands performed signal to the Jew that he/she is a child of the covenant (Qumran, Philo).

Meeks then examines Christian values and beliefs as expressed within the social world described. He suggests that the Christian movement defined itself both positively and negatively, in terms of the "great traditions" of the locally dominant culture. The early Christian communities were affected by their setting and status within the larger empire. Their status affected what they could do (possibilities) and their perception of what they should do (obligations [cf. Meeks 1986:38]).

Finally, Meeks surveys a number of early Christian texts (1 Thessalonians, 1 Corinthians, Matthew, Revelation, Didache, Irenaeus) which seek to affect both the thinking and the behavior of their audiences (Meeks 1986:125). In 1 Thessalonians the moral expectations Paul expresses are very similar to those widely accepted in Greco-Roman society. Yet his concern with holiness emphasizes the distinctiveness and separation of the Christian community from the dominant society (Meeks 1986:129). 1 Corinthians reflects the fact that within early Christianity rules (e.g., regarding idolmeat, fornication) were not so clearly laid out as it seems in Acts 15 (1986:133). Paul's compromise on idol-meat reflects the tensions between the people of different status in the Corinthian church (1986:135).

Meeks has done much to show how various philosophies have impacted early Christianity, particularly in the area of moral instruction (1986:114–19; 1993:66–90; 102–4). Despite this, however, Meeks quickly dismisses the philosophical schools as an analogy for Pauline community formation. He suggests that the Epicurean and Pythagorean groups are like the Pauline communities insofar as they both take the form of modified households or voluntary associations (Meeks 1983:84),[7] but have little else in common with the philosophical schools. The strong scholarly, academic and rhetorical elements within the Pauline groups are ancillary to the primary features of the groups. Ultimately, Meeks seems to favor the synagogue as the best analogy for the early Christian groups (see chapter 1). Nevertheless, his writings provide solid and readable insight into the world of the Hellenistic moral philosophers.

Propagation

In his book, *Conversion* (1933), *A. D. Nock* attempts to determine what it was about Christianity that made it appealing to men and women of antiquity, so much so that they were willing to turn away from previous forms of worship and belong to this new group "body and soul." Nock suggests that the only analogous group in which one can find something akin to "conversion" as it is understood in Judaism and Christianity lies in the philosophical movement. Philosophy held that there was a higher life and a lower life, and philosophical groups attempted to turn persons[8] from the lower to the higher (1933:14). In the Hellenistic age their central interest was primarily ethical (1933:114).

Nock discusses a number of the philosophical schools. In the sixth century B.C.E. the Pythagoreans formed ascetic societies with well-formed doctrines and practices which one entered after a period of preliminary discipline (1933:165). In the fourth century Plato formed the Academy, thus giving the tradition of Socrates a permanent standing. Also discussed are the Stoics, Epicureans and Cynics. In the Hellenistic age such schools held a dominant place for a number of reasons. First, they offered explanations of natural and political phenomena. Second, they offered a way of life which was clearly laid out. Third, philosophy gave rise to men who became "ideal types" for others to follow. Fourth, one could hear an actual philosopher expound his beliefs in public. The adhesion to the teachings and practices of a philosophical school amounted to a "conversion." In all of these aspects Nock finds parallels

in Christianity. Thus, for him, Christianity as a whole is most like a philosophy, and Christian groups were most like philosophical schools (cf.
1933:211; 219).[9]

Contrary to Nock, **Martin Goodman** (1994:32–37) is generally
skeptical that there was any sense of a universal proselytizing mission
by which philosophical ideas were diffused in the Roman Empire.[10] He
argues that while it is clear that philosophers from most of the major
schools of thought sought to change the lives and attitudes of others,
there is little evidence that they sought to have the general population
enter into their own self-defined groups. "Their aim was universal in
scope, but their mission was to educate rather than proselytize"
(1994:37). However, philosophical schools are not his primary concern;
that honor belongs to the synagogues (see chapter 1), and Goodman's
analysis needs further work. Although he may well be correct concerning the lack of a "universalizing proselytizing mission" in the philosophical schools, the approaches that some philosophers used to affect
change in the lives of men and women have proven informative for
understanding Paul's own "mission."

In his 1978 article, "Paul's Tentmaking and the Problem of His
Social Class," **Ronald F. Hock** focuses on Paul the tentmaker. Two important passages that reveal that Paul worked as a tradesman are 1 Corinthians 4:12 ("working with our own hands") and 1 Thessalonians 2:9
("for you remember our labor and toil, brethren; we worked night and
day...."). However, Hock also looks to two other passages to show that
Paul was working at a trade: 1 Corinthians 9:19 and 2 Corinthians 11:7.
In the former, Paul claims freedom from others because he preached the
gospel free of charge. However, in order to do so he worked ("was
enslaved") at his trade. His presence in the workshop, however, brought
about a loss of status, a loss he considered worthwhile for the gaining
of converts through his presence there. In the second passage, Paul's
language indicates that he considered working at a trade demeaning.
Both passages suggest that Paul came from a social status which considered working at a trade "slavish and demeaning," namely, the provin-
cial aristocratic class (1978:562).[11]

In an article published the following year (1979) entitled "The
Workshop as a Social Setting for Paul's Missionary Preaching," Hock
argues that Paul used workshops as settings for his missionary preaching. In so doing, Paul was in keeping with some of the philosophical

teachers of his day (1979:438; cf. 1980:37–41). Drawing on the evidence of both Paul's letters and Acts, Hock makes a strong case for Paul spending time preaching and teaching in workshops, at least as much as in synagogues and households. Hock then looks at the philosophers prior to Paul. Socrates is said to have conversed with Simon the shoemaker in Simon's workshop; tradition also has it that Socrates spent much of his time in a variety of workshops (Xenophon, *Memorabilia Socratis* 4.2.1–39; 3.10.1–15) and in the marketplace (Plato, *Apologia* 17C). In this way, philosophical discourse was kept open and public. It became less so when Plato and Antisthenes chose to teach in the gymnasia.

The Cynics are the one group of philosophers whose teaching remained open and public at all times. They chose the marketplace as the place of discourse, although there are some traditions which place them in the workshops of various artisans (Hock 1979:446). In fact, the Cynics themselves were not adverse to working—Simon the shoemaker is turned, in the tradition, into an ideal Cynic philosopher, his work allowing him "self-sufficiency" and his workshop providing the location for philosophical discourse.

Hock then suggests that, in the tradition of the Cynic preachers, Paul would have used his time in the workshop to both work and preach/teach. Thus he was able to support himself and carry on his missionary activity (citing 1 Thess 2:9). His audience would have been composed of fellow workers, customers and perhaps curious onlookers who had heard of the newly arrived "tentmaker-philosopher." From this group, Hock suggests, the more curious would return for individual instruction (1 Thess 2:11–12), eventually converting to Christianity (1 Thess 2:13).

In his book, *The Social Context of Paul's Ministry* (1980), Hock gives more complete supporting evidence for the conclusions of his two articles, suggesting that Paul was an aristocrat who chose to ply a trade and that he effectively used his location in the workshop to preach, teach and make disciples. In the book he describes well the life of the artisan-missionary, including its many hardships (1980:26–37).

Hock shows how Paul might have related to the intellectual milieu of his day as an artisan-philosopher. Yet in neither of the articles nor his book does Hock go on to describe what sort of community would be formed from this type of missionary preaching—would it be a philosophical school or a workers guild? If all converts were fellow tradesmen and their families, then one could envision the Christian community being formed like the trade associations (see chapter 4). However, if it were a mixed group, then it might more resemble a philosophical school.[12]

Philosophical Schools as a Model

In his 1971 article, "Collegia, Philosophical Schools and Theology," **Robert Wilken** traces the origins of the specific identification of Christianity as a philosophical school to Justin (d. ca. 165 C.E.). However, "few of his contemporaries and none of his predecessors would have felt at all comfortable with such an understanding of Christianity" (1971:274). This identification is also found in the writings of Galen (b. ca. 130 C.E.). To Galen, Christianity was a philosophical school, albeit of a "second or third rate" sort (1971:277). Yet, while Galen did not agree with the teachings of the Christians, he did accord Christianity respect on a par with that given to other philosophical schools (1984:73). Nevertheless, Galen was almost alone in attributing the title of "philosophical school" to the Christian groups. Most people did not consider them to be such.

Wilken is not arguing that Christian groups were organized along the same lines as philosophical schools. Rather, he is pointing out that during the second century, both Christian (Justin Martyr; Melito, Bishop of Sardis) and non-Christian (Galen) commentators used the model of the philosophical school to explain the phenomenon of the Christian group. This does not indicate whether the claim is true or false, but that the analogy was at least helpful to some in antiquity. Nevertheless, later in the article Wilken nuances this somewhat by suggesting that since the Christian groups were also seen as voluntary associations (see chapter 4), they were actually a combination of both philosophical school and voluntary association.

In fact, few scholars argue directly that Paul formed a philosophical school. However, **Hans Conzelmann** (1966:307; 315, n. 95; 1965:233) is one of those few. He suggests that Paul (along with Apollos) founded and operated a philosophical school with a "theological faculty" that trained others for the expansion of Christianity. This school, he suggests, was located in Ephesus (cf. Acts 19:9) and continued on after the death of Paul, eventually producing its own literature (such as Colossians and Ephesians). However, Conzelmann presents little evidence for the structure of the school or contemporary analogies (Meeks 1983:82), and thus has not been favorably received. Nevertheless, a number of scholars argue that Paul used the strategies and language of the philosophers and, in some cases, this leads directly to the inference that Paul conceived of Christianity as a philosophical school—not just another philosophical school, but the school where the aims and goals of the moral philosophers would be fulfilled in Christ.

In his book (1960b), *The Social Pattern of Christian Groups in the First Century, E. A. Judge* seems at first to favor voluntary associations as the best analogy for understanding the Pauline groups (see chapter 4). However, he seems to have quickly shifted towards favoring philosophical schools (without rejecting other possibilities outright). In a separate study published in the same year, he suggests that Paul and his followers were "sophists" who organized local groups into "scholastic communities" which pursued an "intellectual mission" and often resembled a "debating society" (Judge 1960a; Meeks 1983:82). However, Judge does admit that this model alone is not enough to explain how the communities were formed and organized, as this is untypical of other sophists of the time (Judge 1960a:135). Paul is parallel to philosophical preachers in that both have a love of words and of teaching. Paul is a "sophist" or touring lecturer who was invited into public places (cf. Acts) or houses. Paul also had an interest in ethical issues.

In a later work he suggests that when Paul withdrew from the synagogue in each city, his activities must have been carried out under the aegis of some accepted social convention or institution (Judge 1972:32). Since Paul reflects vigorous talk and argument about behaviors and ideas, Judge suggests that philosophy, perhaps even the sophistic movement, can be seen as the social setting for Paul's ministry. However, he rejects the Stoic-Cynic diatribe as a valid background for understanding Paul. In his epistolary techniques Paul has some similarities to the diatribe, but no more than one would expect from persons who share a common milieu. The diatribe

> deals in commonplaces, delivered as a literary creation against stock targets. It lacks altogether the engagement with actual people, circumstances and disputed ideas that is characteristic of Paul. (1972:33)

Rather than being a "regular system of thought," Paul's writings represent "a loose body of general principles for life" such as often "develops amongst thoughtful people in community" (1972:33). This is not to suggest that Paul is operating a disciplined philosophical school, although his groups "may draw from them" (1972:33).

Judge's rejection of the "Stoic-Cynic" diatribe as a background goes back to *Rudolf Bultmann* (1910), who was one of the first to compare Paul's preaching style with the Cynic-Stoic diatribe. However, his emphasis was on the public oral preaching of Paul (and the philosophers) and not on the resultant community which was founded.[13] For Bultmann (and others), the diatribe was "a form of mass propaganda which used various sorts of dialogical and rhetorical techniques in order to create interest and persuade the common man on the street" (Stowers 1981:175). It was used by the itinerant Cynic and Stoic philosophers to spread their message broadly.

More recently, however, *Stanley K. Stowers* (1981; 1988) has argued that the older conception of the "Cynic-Stoic" diatribe is inadequate. Instead, the designation "diatribe" should be reserved for "teaching activity in the schools, literary imitations of that activity, or for writings which employ the rhetorical and pedagogical type typical of diatribes in the schools" (Stowers 1988:73; cf. 1981:76). Paul's use of the diatribe suggests that he entered into the student-teacher relationship similar to the situation of the philosophical school.[14] Paul's use of the diatribe not only shows his familiarity with the discourse style of the popular philosophers of his day, but also suggests that he attempted to establish his communities on the model of the teacher-student relationship of the philosophical schools. His letter to the Romans reflects the way Paul preached, not in order to make converts, but in order to teach those who had already committed themselves to his way of life. In fact, Stowers refers to Paul's fellow workers (especially those mentioned in Rom 16) as his former "students." Those in Rome will provide "a more personal introduction for Paul as a teacher to the church at Rome" (1981:183). In fact, Paul uses the diatribe style when writing his letter to the Romans in order to introduce and prepare them for the school he will form in Rome upon his arrival there.

David E. Aune argues that Paul's letter to the Romans is a *logos protreptikos* (1991). This type of lecture or "speech of exhortation" was used by philosophers to attract people to their way of life. The primary setting for the *logos protreptikos* was the philosophical school. Thus, if Paul is using this form of Greco-Roman philosophical argument, then it implies that he does so with an understanding that Christianity is much like a philosophical school, and that he himself is one of the leading philosophers (Aune 1991:279).[15] Certainly this is the implication given throughout Aune's article (see esp. 1991:286–87).

The *logos protreptikos* was an oral or literary genre used by many philosophers to encourage a listener to convert to the philosopher's particular way of life. Included in the genre was the strong dissuasion or censure of the audience's current beliefs and practices followed by the positive demonstration of the value and profit of the particular philosophy. Often a personal appeal might conclude the argument. Many examples of this type of philosophic propaganda exist from antiquity, some of which Aune summarizes. One of the most interesting is that of Lucian, a second century C.E. satirist who uses the genre in four instances of conversion. Once he uses a *logos protreptikos* in a dialogue which ends with the conversion of Lucian himself (*Nigrinus*), while three other dialogues are parodies of *logoi protreptikoi* (*Hermotimus, De parasito, De saltatione*).

Turning to Romans itself, Aune points out that there is little agreement among scholars as to the proper generic designation of Romans. Aune suggests that the central section of Romans (1:16–15:13) is a *logos protreptikos* set within an epistolary framework (1:1–15 and 15:14–16:27). The nature of the material suggests that Paul "worked and reworked this material over a period of several years" (1991:290). In fact, the material reflects a number of separate *logoi protreptikoi* used and developed by Paul in his oral teaching and preaching (1991:296). These have been linked together by Paul "to form a relatively coherent *logos protreptikos* in their present context in Romans" (1991:296). Three of the four primary sections argue with various groups with whom Paul would dialogue on a regular basis: pagans (1:18–2:11), Jews (2:12–4:25) and Christians (5:1–8:39). In recounting these *logoi protreptikoi* Paul is not only showing the Roman Christians how he presents the gospel in various settings, but he is also presenting to them his gospel (since Paul had never visited the Roman congregations). Unfortunately, Romans 9–11 does not fit the genre so well, but Aune suggests that it functions as a digression on the problem of Jewish unbelief, with attendant Old Testament exegesis. While not a *logos protreptikos* it does reflect Paul's use of another Hellenistic school feature—the exegesis of authoritative texts. The examples of moral behavior found in Romans 12:1–15:13 form the concluding paraenetic section of the larger *logos protreptikos* that is Romans.

Aune's work is supported by the more recent study of ***Anthony J. Guerra, Romans and the Apologetic Tradition*** (1995). Guerra argues that Paul wrote Romans as a protreptic letter for a number of reasons. First, he attempts to teach his Law-free gospel to Gentiles and address objections from Jewish Christians. At the same time, he hopes to garner support for his trip to Spain. Second, Paul is attempting to mediate between the Jewish and Gentile factions within the Roman community, thus avoiding the civil disturbances which had earlier led to the expulsion of the Jews (49 C.E.).

Guerra attempts to show how each of the major sections of Romans has a function within the *logos protreptikos*. Romans 1:18–3:31 (and Rom 14–15) is full of apologetic motifs affirming the full inclusion of the Gentiles in the church and assuring the Jewish Christians that Paul's preaching is not blasphemous. In Romans 4 Paul uses Abraham as a testimonial figure and as scriptural confirmation that God acts in a manner consistent with past promises. Romans 5 through 8 function within the protreptic as demonstrations of the value and profit of the philosophy (Christianity) by commending the life made possible in Christ. In Romans 9 through 11 Paul takes up the negative aspect of protreptic by countering alternative proposals to his gospel and ministry. Finally, in Romans 12, 13 and 16 Paul attempts to convince the Roman Christians that he is a loyal subject of the Emperor and will not bring them into disrepute when he arrives in Rome, thus showing Christianity as a preferred way of life.

Although not in full agreement on the details of Paul's protreptic in Romans, the works of Aune and Guerra do suggest that in using the genre of *logos protreptikos* Paul is not only aligned with the Hellenistic philosophers, but views the Christian communities themselves as philosophical "schools," and thus appropriate settings for certain types of oral and literary activity such as the *logoi protreptikoi.*

The Epicureans provide an obvious analogy to early Christian groups since there were thriving Epicurean communities throughout the Roman Empire (De Lacy 1948). Epicurus lived from 341 to 270 B.C.E. Although born on Samos, he settled in Athens and established a school of philosophy there called "the Garden." Although this was a "commune," there was no pooling of resources, and, unlike other schools of philosophy, women and slaves were admitted on a par with men. Epicurus aimed to teach people how to be happy, aptly summarized in the so-called "four-part cure": "Don't fear god, Don't worry about death; What is good is easy to get, and What is terrible is easy to endure" (Inwood, Gerson, Hutchinson 1994:vii). His teachings were attractive to many people, and groups of "Epicureans" continued to exist after his death and well into the Common Era. In many ways Epicureanism was less a philosophical system than it was a cult of the founder. Followers assumed that Epicurus had discovered the only true way to live life (De Witt 1936:205; Simpson 1941:378–79).

One of the foremost advocates of using Epicureanism for understanding Pauline communities is ***Norman De Witt.***[16] De Witt's book on *St. Paul and Epicurus* (1954b) is the sequel to his *Epicurus and His Philosophy* (1954a). In the earlier book De Witt dropped a number of hints that Paul drew heavily on Epicurean philosophy. In fact, in his later book he suggests that in his pre-Christian life Paul had himself been educated as an Epicurean (1954b:168).

The later book is De Witt's attempt to show where Paul draws on his knowledge of Epicureanism. In some instances Paul uses Epicurean words and phrases in Christian contexts, betraying his indebtedness to it. In other instances Paul is reacting against the Epicurean Christians in his community, thus denigrating the philosophy. De Witt examines a broad cross-section of Paul's writings, particularly Philippians, 1 Thessalonians, Galatians, and 1 Corinthians. He also includes chapters on Ephesians and Colossians, and his text is interspersed with references to other Pauline and deutero-Pauline letters, including the pastorals.

De Witt highlights a number of commonalities between Paul and Epicureans: they both drew from the middle classes of society; they were both missionary oriented and both were concerned with "peace and safety" (cf. 1 Thes 5:3). Paul also shows familiarity with the Canon of Epicurus as well as his physics and ethics. In particular, De Witt points to Paul's warnings against the "elements of the universe" (Gal 4:3, 9; Col 2:8, 20; cf. Heb 5:12; 2 Pt 3:10, 12)[17] as a direct attack on Epicurean atomic physics, which held that the universe consists of atoms and space. When he examines individual letters of Paul, De Witt finds in each a number of phrases which resonate with Epicurean vocabulary and thinking, and ways of reasoning found in the writings of Epicurus. All of this leads him to posit the direct influence of the writings of Epicurus and the practices of Epicureanism on the apostle Paul.

While dealing primarily with the language of Paul in his letters, De Witt does suggest that the formation of Epicurean communities was the prototype for the formation of Christian communities. Paul, like the followers of Epicurus, gathered together followers of the initial teacher in order to perpetuate the memory of that teacher. For the Epicureans it was Epicurus; for Paul it was Jesus the Christ. Both groups revered their founder as the discoverer of truth and as savior (1954b:vi). Both groups were formed from private households.[18]

Not only were Epicureans and Christians similar in using household-based groups, these groups could be formed as schools. Again, the concept originated with the Epicureans and was copied by the Christians (1954b:97).[19] De Witt suggests that some aspects of the organizational structure of the Christian groups are based on that of Epicurean groups. He even claims that Epicurus's habit of writing pastoral letters to his communities must have been the model for Paul's letter writing, as "no other model existed" (1944:255). By the late first century the Christian groups became the chief rivals of the Epicurean groups, eventually supplanting them. By the fifth century the Epicureans had been absorbed into the Christian community (1954a:328).

De Witt's suggestions of Paul's use of Epicurean philosophy can be described variously as plausible, improbable, fanciful and downright wrong. In fact, De Witt's books were not well received (most notably by Schmid 1962). So opposed were many to De Witt's suggestions that they discounted the possibility of a philosophical background to Paul's letters completely. However, as Malherbe points out, De Witt's excesses should not disqualify more responsible attempts (Malherbe 1989a:15).

In *Paul and Philodemus: Adaptability in Epicurean and Early*

Christian Psychagogy (1995), **Clarence E. Glad** has pursued the comparison of the Epicurean school and Pauline Christian groups in a more nuanced, and perhaps more successful way. Glad suggests that Paul's "psychagogic" practice, his style of caring for his community, has affinities with that of the Epicureans, particularly those Epicurean schools at Athens, Naples and Herculaneum in the mid-first century B.C.E.[20] Of the possible models available, Glad's emphasis on the psychagogic aspects of Paul's community "favors the model of the philosophical school" (1995:8–9 n. 15). However, this does not mean that there is direct influence or borrowings, only that there is a common communal practice. In both communities, the Pauline and the Epicurean, there is a pattern of "mutual participation by community members in exhortation, edification and correction" (1995:8). Yet this pattern is important as a defining characteristic of the community; "it establishes a form of community ethos which binds members together in their common purpose" (1995:11). In fact, this "participatory psychagogy" "is a defining and constitutive feature of both Epicurean and proto-Christian communities" (1995:335). Paul is not innovative in his approach to community education. Rather, he uses the approach found in the Epicurean schools.

Glad spends the first two chapters giving an overview of the tradition of psychagogic nurture in antiquity. The ancient orator along with the moral counselor or guide would have to be prepared to be adaptable and versatile when faced with audiences composed of people of different dispositions and backgrounds. An entire pool of hortatory techniques was needed on which one could draw if necessary. These psychagoges, or "mature guides," were often sought out by people in antiquity as a source of guidance for life. The type of guidance offered was mixed, both harsh and gentle, as the situation required.

When Glad turns to Epicurean psychagogy he finds his best example in the works of Philodemus, especially his *On Frank Criticism*. And it is precisely in Philodemus that Glad finds the best match when it comes to community guidance. By analyzing both Philodemus and Paul, he concludes that both recognize the twofold perspective of frank speech (harsh and gentle), the importance of friendship and the community-wide use of exhortation, edification and correction (1995:105; cf. 107, 185, 193, 204). Although Glad shows how this approach is worked out in Romans 14:1 through15:14 (1995:213–35), his principal focus is the Corinthian community. He suggests that to the weak and insecure Paul's approach is mild or gentle. However, when faced with a recalcitrant person, Paul's approach is much more harsh. As with Epicurean psychagogy, Paul's approach takes into account the disposition and background of the recipient of the moral guidance. In so doing, Paul became "all things to all people" or as Glad translates it "I have become every thing in turn to men of every sort" (1 Cor 9:22b).

Another popular philosophical school during the first century C.E., along with the Epicureans, is that of the Stoics (cf. Acts 17:18). Stoicism was founded in Athens by Zeno of Citium, who lived during the fourth and third centuries B.C.E. Zeno first converted to Cynicism under Crates and then turned to Socratic philosophy before developing his own philosophy. He first expounded his philosophy in the stoa in Athens, hence the name of the philosophical system. Eventually he organized a school in Athens, which continued until Justinian closed all of the Athenian philosophical schools in 529 C.E. During that lengthy period Stoicism underwent much development and change, beginning with Zeno's successor, Chrysippus, who sought to systematize Zeno's ideas. Stoicism was well received in the Roman world and included amongst its adherents Cicero, Seneca, Epictetus and Marcus Aurelius.

Stoics held that the whole universe is controlled by reason (*logos*), which is identified with God and shows itself as fate. The role of the wise person is to live in harmony with whatever happens, knowing that it cannot be changed—one must live with indifference to everything. Humans obtain true freedom by living consistently with nature, putting aside passion, unjust thoughts, indulgence and the like and performing one's duties with the right disposition. This is the goal—the virtuous life.

Investigation of Stoicism as a background for Pauline community formation has also proved fruitful, particularly in the recent essay of **Troels Engberg-Pedersen,** "Stoicism in Philippians" (1995).[21] Although Engberg-Pedersen states at the outset that Paul was not a Stoic philosopher, he shows convincingly how Paul carefully integrates Stoic ideas in his letter to the Philippians. Unlike other studies which simply show Stoic ideas in Paul, Engberg-Pedersen ties Paul's Stoicizing motifs directly to the community formation of the Philippians. Paul's Stoic referents suggest that, consciously or not, Paul is attempting to form a community of a special kind.

Zeno, in his *Republic,* envisioned a particular ideal community that could arise out of Stoic teaching, where all distinctions based on social rank, gender, political affiliation and the like were abolished. No hierarchies would be in place and all people would have the freedom to engage in independent action. Of course, the wise person would choose to do what was morally good. Following Zeno, this conception of the ideal community was slightly modified. First, vestiges of Cynicism were removed. Second, and more importantly, under Chrysippus the community changed from a locally based population center to "a community of all those people who are morally good wherever they live on earth" (1995:267). It is this later development that is most relevant to Paul.

Engberg-Pedersen shows how a number of terms and concepts found in Philippians are used with the meaning they have within the writings of Stoic philosophers. He then takes note of other dominant motifs in Philippians such as the coming judgment on the "day of Christ" and *koinōnia,* the conception that people will care for others because they consider them above themselves. He suggests that Paul's argument for Christian *politeuma* ("citizenship") in heaven (Phil 3:20) reflects the basic ideas of Stoic moral and political philosophy: that there is an end or goal towards which this life is aiming, and that this end is an ideal community which must be realized as much as possible in present circumstances by one's beliefs and behavior. While Paul elaborates on this based on his understanding of Christian life, in his community-forming enterprise "Paul is actually using Stoicism" (1995:279).[22]

Loveday Alexander, "Paul and the Hellenistic Schools" (1995), follows the work of Nock (1933) who, as we have seen above, suggests that to the ancient observer the synagogue and the church would have most resembled the philosophical school. Drawing on the writings of Galen, a second-century medical doctor who was enamored of neither the philosophical schools nor of Christianity, Alexander shows how Christianity (and Judaism) was simply assumed to be another philosophical school. Galen seems to suggest in one passage that the "followers of Moses and Christ" are no worse, and may even be better, than adherents of the philosophical schools. Galen's observation must be based on the teaching activities and the traditions of the Jews and Christians (1995:67).

Like the philosophical schools, Christian groups based their identity on the authority of the founding figure (1995:72). They were less concerned with academic and rational thought than is often assumed; rather, their adherents conducted both private and public lectures on their own positions, often advocating uncritical devotion to the school and its founder (1995:77). The teachers from the schools used a variety of locations and styles for presenting their message. In this way, Paul is very much like them. He is able to travel around the Mediterranean, speaking in public places and private dwellings.

Alexander's is very much a preliminary foray into the debate, and she pulls back at the end of the essay by suggesting both that other analogies might be apt (e.g., trade guilds; 1995:79) and that her analysis only establishes the model of the school as an important tool (1995:81–82). In the end, however, she discounts the trade guilds by suggesting that, unlike the schools, the guilds did not produce literature nor did they see themselves as part of a worldwide movement.[23] Presumably, the philosophical schools remain as the most adequate "tool" for understanding early Christian groups.

Conclusion

It should be clear from the discussion in this chapter that while many scholars find in the Hellenistic moral philosophers an appropriate background for understanding Paul's thought and language, only a few articulate the extension of this to an understanding of how Paul organized his communities. Nevertheless, by implication many would have to grant that by addressing his communities as if they were as familiar as himself with the nuances of various philosophical systems, Paul is assuming that they would understand themselves in light of the model of the philosophical "schools." Yet, since there is no one dominant philosophical system in evidence, and because of the diversity among the "schools" themselves, this understanding quickly begins to break down. One of the most sustained arguments for Pauline Christian communities being (Epicurean) philosophical schools has not been well received (that of De Witt). Yet, for the continued use of the philosophical systems as a background for Paul's thought, what New Testament scholarship now needs is a sustained examination of both the nature and extent of the formation and organization of the philosophical schools themselves, followed by a detailed examination of analogous material in Paul's letters.

3
The Ancient Mysteries

Paul and the Mysteries[1]

In Romans 6:1–11 Paul describes how Christians have undergone the rite of baptism. These verses have been used to suggest that Paul received his baptismal theology from the mysteries. In fact, this passage is often the "entry point" for arguing in favor of the influence of the mysteries on Paul's theology and Paul's communities (Wedderburn 1982:824).[2] Paul's description of the process reads like this:

> Do you not know that all of us who have been baptized into Christ Jesus were baptized into his death? We were buried therefore with him by baptism into death, so that as Christ was raised from the dead by the glory of the Father, we too might walk in newness of life. (Rom 6:3–4)

As we shall see, the idea of dying and rising with Christ is said to come directly from the mysteries (cf. Wedderburn 1987b:57).

Other texts are also thought to reflect the influence of the mysteries on Paul. For example, *R. E. Witt* (1971; cf. 1966a:137–38; 1966b: 53–54, 58, 61) has pointed out a number of interesting, albeit disparate, parallels between the deeds (in Acts) and letters attributed to Paul and the cult of Isis. Details from Paul's letters are taken to indicate that Paul must have come into contact with the Isiac faith. For example, Paul's key theological terms, "power" and "salvation," have parallels in the Isis cult; his attack on the anthropomorphism and zoolatry of depraved humans in Romans 1:23 might be a direct attack on the iconography of the Egyptian cults; mention of sounding brass and a tinkling cymbal in 1 Corinthians 13 brings to mind the music made by Isis in renewing the earth in midwinter (1971:266); the "name above all names" attributed to Jesus in the Philippian hymn (Phil 2:9) plays off the many great names of the goddess Isis, the "Queen Victoria" of the Roman colony of Philippi (1971:267–68; cf. 1966b:61).

As these examples show, Witt is suggesting that Paul was by no means sympathetic to the cult of Isis. While much of his language might resonate with the language of that cult (e.g., *eucharistia, ekklēsia;* 1971:268), in fact Paul was critical of it. Paul's fundamental belief in a male deity, his monotheism, his Christology and his patriarchy all prevented him from adopting too much from the cult of Isis. In a separate article (1966a), Witt uses a similar methodology (that of finding "parallels") to suggest that the cult of Isis had a profound influence on the beliefs and liturgical practices of the Christian church during the patristic period despite the disclaimers of the church fathers themselves.

Nature and Extent of Mysteries

Description

The mysteries were "initiation rituals of a voluntary, personal and secret character that aimed at a change of mind through experience of the sacred" (Burkert 1987:11). An individual initiate might then also be joined with other initiates to form an association in which members would participate together in certain secret rites under the patronage of a particular deity. The mysteries tended to emphasize salvation for individuals who chose to be initiated into the mysteries, resulting in groups of believers who were inwardly focused (Meyer 1992:941). Although they had some public celebrations such as processions and sacrifices, they emphasized the secret ceremonies, only known to the initiates (Meyer 1992:941). The emphasis in the mystery rites (of which little is now known) seems to have been on the experience rather than the imparting of information (Meyer 1992:941). The rites themselves were thought to bring about certain benefits, especially after the death of the initiate (Wedderburn 1987b:56–57; Ferguson, 1987:198).

The mysteries have a long history. One of the earliest mysteries was that of Demeter and Kore at Eleusis, which extends back at least to the sixth century B.C.E. The mysteries of Dionysus appear only slightly later than this (Burkert 1987:2). The propensity for mysteries grew in the Hellenistic age and even more so in the Roman period, probably due to the contact of western peoples with these predominantly eastern religions through war, trade and travel. Some of the most important mysteries at this time include those of Dionysus, the Great Mother (Cybele) and Attis, Isis and Sarapis (Osiris), and Mithras.

Unfortunately, space does not allow us to give the details of each here. We would caution, however, that it is no longer adequate, as we shall see, to treat the mysteries as a homogeneous entity, and thus generalize about mystery "theology" or mystery "practice." Such generalizations have led others into improper comparisons with Christianity. Each of the mysteries must be investigated on its own terms, using its own terminology, as far as this is known.[3] For a description of the major mysteries and the contours of their beliefs, a brief but thorough guide is Luther H. Martin's *Hellenistic Religions* (1987) or Walter Burkert's *Ancient Mystery Cults* (1987).[4]

Despite the above disclaimer, the mysteries did share some general characteristics (Meyer 1992:941) that we might briefly mention here. The mysteries were rooted in the soil, agriculture and the cycle of nature. Their rites aimed to assure fertility and safety, although they also promised a happy afterlife. For the most part, they tended to be of a voluntary nature (Stambaugh and Balch 1986:132; cf. Bultmann 1956: 157). The initiation ceremony was collective, not individual, but the choice to receive initiation into a mystery was individual. Thus, the mysteries were an expression of personal religion (Ferguson 1987:197).

There is evidence for three forms of organization for the practice of the mysteries (see Burkert 1987:30–53 for details). The first was the individual itinerant or charismatic practitioner who wandered around the circum-Mediterranean as a prophet and a seer in the name of a deity, but who was not aligned with a particular group. The second type of organization was based upon a sanctuary, either as part of the civic administration of the city or on family property, with attendant priests and/or priestesses. During the late Hellenistic and Roman period most of the well-established mysteries had sanctuaries, professional priests and sacred symbols and rites, although the practice of these mysteries was not limited to these locations. The third type of organization was that of the voluntary association, whose focus was a particular deity and its affiliated mysteries.[5] In the latter two forms, the association of initiates could participate in a number of communal events, including meals and banquets, dances and ceremonies, especially the initiation rites. All three types of social manifestations were not mutually exclusive. For example, an itinerant may have decided to form an association of initiates, or a local public sanctuary might have had a private voluntary association attached to it (Burkert 1987:32).

Propagation

Martin Goodman (1994:32) has provided a nice, concise summary of the missionizing efforts of Greco-Roman cults generally. Since most of his examples are from the mysteries, it is perhaps apropos to quote it in detail here:

> In sum, attitudes to mission varied greatly in ancient polytheism. When it occurred, mission was usually apologetic and propagandistic. The many inscriptions found in shrines proclaiming to passersby the power and benevolence of the divinity may be included in these categories; their prime aim was simply to praise the god, on the assumption that the gods, like men, love to be honored. Only occasionally did the adherents of a cult with a particular awareness of the significance of its geographical spread, such as the advocates of emperor worship, indulge in proselytizing. Even in their case there is no evidence that their ambitions were universalist in scope. No pagan seriously dreamed of bringing all humankind to give worship in one body to one deity.

Despite this judgment, however, there is some evidence of the propagation of the mysteries, albeit a limited amount. One of the most obvious mysteries in which we find propagation is that of Mithras.

Through its adherents among the traders and soldiers of antiquity, the cult of Mithras was able to traverse the Roman Empire from the eastern regions of its origin to Rome and beyond in the west (see Teeple 1988:317). However, Goodman is certainly correct in suggesting that there was no large-scale effort among the mysteries to propagate their faith. And yet, they all seemed to attract adherents despite this. It is important to note that initiation into the mysteries did not necessarily mean that one had "converted" to another religion. One could be initiated into more than one of the mysteries and participate in the rites associated with each.

The Mysteries as a Model

Older Advocates

From as early as the church fathers, commentators, both Christian and non-Christian alike, have noted the similarities between Christianity and the mysteries.[7] For the most part, the early Christians insisted that Christianity developed independently of the mysteries. Any similarities were due to the work of demons anticipating Christianity and having certain Christian rites copied in the mysteries.[8]

One of the first modern scholars to indicate that Christianity was influenced by the mysteries was Isaac Casaubon in 1614, who suggested that the mysteries were the source of the Christian sacraments (Teeple 1992:51; Metzger 1968:1 n. 1). The first scholar to undertake a more critical investigation of the mysteries themselves was C. A. Lobeck in 1829, who was able to clear the way for a more scientific study of the mysteries (Metzger 1968:1). His work was followed by that of Gustav Anrich in 1894, who brought to the comparative investigation a comprehensiveness and precision in methodology not previously encountered (Wagner 1967:7).

The use of the mysteries as an analogy for understanding early Christianity peaked under the influence of the history-of-religions school (German *religionsgeschichtliche Schule*) of the late nineteenth and early twentieth century.[9] **Richard Reitzenstein's** *Hellenistic Mystery-Religions* (1910, ET 1978)[10] is seen as a prime example of the approach of this history-of-religions school. He compares a number of disconnected mystery works to arrive at the general features of the missionary activities of the mystery cults. He argues that before undertaking his own missionizing program, Paul carried out a systematic study of the language and concepts of the mysteries (1978:536). As a result, Paul's view of baptism and the Lord's Supper was directly influenced by the rites of initiation in the mysteries (1978:76–81).[11] In fact, this study continued to help Paul as he attempted to communicate effectively with the communities with which he was associated (1978:85, 536), suggesting that Paul's communities themselves were made up of those familiar with mystery concepts and thus were structured in a similar manner.[12]

In an article from the early part of this century on "The Christian Mystery," *Alfred Loisy* (1911–12) boldly sets out to show that Christianity is not a sect of Judaism but an independent religion. This was not the original intent of the historical Jesus; rather, it came about largely due to the action of Paul. Because of his own background, Paul turned the Gospel of Jesus into a Hellenistic mystery cult.

In describing some of the practices of the mysteries, Loisy makes liberal use of terminology that has a specifically Christian resonance to it. For example, he describes part of the initiation into the cult of Isis and Sarapis (Osiris) in this way:

> As Osiris was plunged in the waters of the Nile in order to revive him, so the novice receives a baptism whereby he is regenerated. He does not merely see the death and resurrection of Osiris in figure; he himself enters into the sacred drama, with a principal part to play; he becomes Osiris....
> (1911:48)

And again, in describing the rites of Cybele and Attis he notes that Attis's "passion and resurrection were duly celebrated" and that, following the rite of anointing with oil, "is found the bloody baptism of the taurobole, which was also a sacrament of regeneration and of immortality" (1911:48).

No wonder, then, that when he turns to Paul he finds analogous material and can suggest that Paul's Christianity was "conceived in its general lines on the same model as those of which we have just been speaking" (1911:50). However, as many people have subsequently pointed out, much of what Loisy describes is not actually present in any of the texts from antiquity. Instead, Loisy has filled in the gaps using language taken from Christianity. Edwyn Bevan pointedly states, "[o]n this plan, you first put in the Christian elements, and then are staggered to find them there" (cited in Metzger 1968:9).

Returning to Loisy, he begins with a brief analysis of Paul's soteriology primarily as it is outlined in Romans. He shows how Jesus is conceived as a savior-god like Sarapis, Attis or Mithras in his appearance on earth, his "universal redemption," his violent death and subsequent return to life and his predetermined plan to involve his followers in his worship in such a way that leads to their salvation. These affinities are nowhere more clear than in the two Christian sacraments of baptism and the Lord's Supper. In Christian baptism the initiate "is held to die in order to be reborn, as in the pagan mysteries" (1911:53). And in the Lord's Supper the elements of wine and bread mystically become the blood and body of Christ, leading to a mystic participation of the celebrant with Christ, a notion stemming directly from the mysteries. It is through this sharing in mystic rites that those who partake "come into or are maintained in the social body of Christ, the community of his believers" (1911:55). For Loisy, the mysteries provide the paradigm for Paul to adapt in his own community formation.

Having suggested that Paul transformed Jesus' gospel into a mystery cult, Loisy concludes by pointing out how this transformation occurred.[13] He suggests that Paul had access to the mystical literature of paganism and had studied it both before his conversion to Christianity and afterwards (1911:58). Having grown up in Tarsus, where the mysteries were known, he would also have had opportunity to encounter their practices and beliefs. In fact, Loisy suggests that Paul also became familiar with the mysteries through his discussions with pagans while attempting to convert them to Judaism. Once he experienced his Christian conversion, he studied the mysteries all the more "in order to acquaint himself with the religious ideas of the races he would win, to find rules for the organization and worship of the communities he would found" (1911:58). However, Paul's Christian communities went beyond the mystic groups, which had no internal cohesion or reciprocal bonds, in that they became stronger in their unity of belief and in their social organization. This factor worked together with firmer theological convictions about God and immortality and a closer tie to the savior-god to allow Christianity to supplant the mysteries and finally to eliminate them (1911:64).

Today Loisy's approach seems simplistic. Most of the parallels he draws between Christianity and the mysteries are superficial at best. In fact, Loisy falls into many of the methodological traps that Metzger would later caution against (1968; see below). However, this did not prevent Loisy from pursuing his thesis, and a similar approach to the common features in the mysteries and early Christianity can be found in his *Les mystères païens et le mystère chrétien* (1914 [*Pagan Mysteries and the Christian Mystery*]; Kee 1995b:145).

In 1913 **Wilhelm Bousset** published a comprehensive and fascinating book called *Kyrios Christos* in which he traces the development of Christianity from its Palestinian beginnings through to the time of Irenaeus at the end of the second century.[14] Bousset's thesis was that Jesus was first addressed as "Lord," not in the early Palestinian community but in the Hellenistic communities. The use of the title *Kyrios* (Greek: "Lord") is drawn from its use for the gods of the mysteries, such as "the Lord Sarapis" or "the Lord Attis."

Having first investigated the primitive Palestinian Christian community, Bousset turns his attention to Hellenistic communities themselves. He sees a significant disjuncture between these two main branches of early Christianity. Although Paul is Jewish, Bousset maintains that much of his theology and practice was influenced by the Hellenistic, not the Palestinian, communities in which he was ministering. In fact, Bousset maintains that Paul did not create the Hellenistic communities from nothing. Many of them were established before Paul's career as apostle to the Gentiles began, especially the influential communities at Antioch and Rome.

Beginning with an investigation of the title *Kyrios,* Bousset suggests that it is used in the Hellenistic churches in place of the Palestinian church's title "Son of Man," since the latter would not be understood among the Gentiles of the Hellenistic churches. Since the title *Kyrios* is absent from the Palestinian traditions embedded in the gospel accounts, the Hellenistic church must have appropriated the use of the title from elsewhere—namely, the mysteries.

The Hellenistic churches' emphasis on the title *Kyrios* points to the common *cultus* of the Christians (1970:130). The Christians are initiated into the worship life of the church through baptism. Once initiated, they participate in the common meal in honor of the cultic hero, "just as the followers of the Egyptian Serapis come to the table of the Lord Serapis" (1970:131; cf. 134). This emphasis on Jesus as the *Kyrios* did not originate with Paul, but with the community itself; it is the collective expression of the Hellenistic community's consciousness of its cultic hero. Paul's use of the expression simply takes over and builds on what the community itself first appropriated in its worship (1970:146–47).

Even Paul's "mysticism," as it is expressed in his view of Christian identity with Christ through baptism in Romans 6, had its origins in the former beliefs of the Christian communities themselves. "The belief must already have been present that baptism as an act of initiation is a dying and coming to life again, somehow comparable to Christ's death and resurrection" (1970:157; cf. 194). This concept of identification and dying and rising has as its background the mysteries (1970:188). The same holds true for the eating and drinking of the body and blood in the rite of the Lord's Supper. Thus, the members of the Hellenistic Christian communities were most likely formerly initiates of one or another of the mysteries before they became Christians. Upon their conversion, they brought with them many aspects of mystery worship into the Christian worship and fashioned their new communities after the model of the adherents of the mysteries.

Bousset does not suggest that Paul simply took over these aspects of the mysteries as they were mediated through the Hellenistic churches. Rather, Paul reworked many of their ideas and practices in light of his own understanding of the Christ-event. Nevertheless, many of the root ideas remain as the base of Christian community, worship and belief in Paul's letters (1970:167), and dominate in the actual practices of the Hellenistic Christian communities (1970:210).

Similar to Bousset, in *Primitive Christianity in its Contemporary Setting* (1949, ET 1956)[15] **Rudolf Bultmann** held that the Hellenistic church developed independently of the Palestinian church even before Paul's missionary activity. Under the influence of Hellenism and even of Paul himself, Hellenistic Christianity became a syncretistic religion (1956:177). A number of elements of Paul's thought and practice are clearly from the Old Testament. However, other aspects are adopted from elsewhere, such as Stoicism, particularly the idea of Christian freedom (1956:185), and Gnosticism, especially Paul's understanding of the condition of humanity in the world and the transedence of God (1956:189–95).

When the Hellenistic church, and particularly Paul, attempted to describe the redemptive significance of Jesus they used terms derived from the mysteries (1956:196).[16] Jesus himself is conceived as a mystery deity, and those initiated into the community participate in Jesus' death and resurrection though the sacraments of baptism and the Lord's Supper (1956:177, 196). These sacraments were incorporated into the Hellenistic church from the mysteries, although Paul himself also seems to have put his own particular stamp on the understanding of them (for details see Bultmann 1952:140–44 and 311–13 on baptism, and 1952:148–51 and 313–14 on the Lord's Supper). This admission is important for understanding how Bultmann conceives of the nature of the Hellenistic church. He has already suggested that it is precisely the sacraments of baptism and the Lord's Supper that cement the Christians into "an eschatological community" (1956:187; cf. 203). Since the sacraments come primarily from the mysteries, then, in outward appearance, if not in theology, Paul's churches must have looked a lot like mystery cults.

A number of points in Bultmann's analysis are problematic at best. The radical distinction between the Hellenistic church and the Palestinian church has been called into question repeatedly. A much more nuanced view of early "Christianities" is called for. Second, Bultmann's description of the mysteries is at best superficial. Although he admits that differences existed among the separate mysteries, he tends to merge them into one when outlining their beliefs and practices. Also, his conception of the individual mysteries are now clearly recognized as out-of-date and downright incorrect (this is especially true of his description of Mithraism).[17]

Opponents of the Analogy

Overall, the history-of-religions school has not maintained many supporters past the early part of the twentieth century. In fact, their approach experienced opposition from the beginning and has long been in disrepute among most New Testament scholars. As we shall see below, a number of influential voices were raised in opposition to the possibility of Christian borrowing from the mysteries. However, it needs to be reemphasized that the movement "has made us necessarily more cognizant of the larger cultural context in which Christianity took stalk and flourished," and has reminded us that it is impossible for a cultural context not to exert an influence on persons or institutions (Wiens 1980:1258). This has led to the further, much more nuanced exploration of the possibility of mystery influences on Paul and his churches in the modern period. We will return to these after summarizing the assessments of the history-of-religions school's detractors.

With characteristic erudition, *A. D. Nock* dismisses the idea that the mysteries had any influence on the Christian sacraments: "Any idea that what we call the Christian sacraments were in their origin indebted to pagan mysteries or even to the metaphorical concepts based upon them shatters on the rock of linguistic evidence" (1972c:809).[18] He suggests that in the initiation rites of the mysteries, washing was merely a preliminary step and nothing like baptism, and a meal was simply a meal, with no special connotations. The one exception is Mithraism, but Nock brushes it aside as being too late to have influenced early Christianity (1972c:810).

Nock clearly rejects the direct influence of the mysteries on Pauline community formation (cf. 1972a:72). In fact, Nock points out the absence from Paul (and the New Testament more generally) of any distinctive terminology from the mysteries (1972c:809–10; 1972e:341–44).[19] That which has in the past been designated as "mystery" terminology is really part of the broader Hellenistic religious vocabulary available to all who lived in that time (1972e:343–44).[20]

Nock was correct when he wrote in 1952 "[u]nless I am mistaken, scholarly opinion is moving towards something like the position which I have outlined" (1972c:819).[21] Within a decade *Günther Wagner* published his *Pauline Baptism and the Pagan Mysteries* (1962, ET 1967),[22] in which he rejected the history-of-religions school approach that sees a "global" understanding of the mysteries and their terminology.[23] In examining Romans 6 and the supposed mystery model behind it, he shows that in fact there is no mystery cult with analogous material

(1967:266). Paul's view developed independently of any influences from the mysteries.

Wagner's book has been "described as the best study of the mystery-religions to have appeared since the early years of this century."[24] However, a more recent investigation of the possible influences of the mysteries on Paul's baptismal language in Romans 6 has been undertaken by *A. J. M. Wedderburn,* with results similar to those of Wagner.[25] Wedderburn makes it clear that he does not think that Pauline communities were directly influenced by the mysteries (1983:337; 1987a:396). He looks in detail at the idea that those initiated into the mysteries shared in the sufferings of a dying and rising god, much like Paul indicates Christians participate in the death and resurrection of Christ through baptism (Rom 6:1–11). Detailed examination of this theme in the various mysteries, however, shows that evidence for this is almost nonexistent (see 1987a:296–331 and in summary form in 1987b:57–71).

Wedderburn is more inclined to see that the similarities between Paul's view of baptism and the mysteries comes more generally from a shared milieu than direct dependence (1987a:393–94). He suggests that the influence was most likely mediated through Hellenistic Judaism (1982:823, 828–29; 1983:337; 1987a:163). In fact, he suggests that "the interpretation of Paul's doctrine of union with Christ as a derivative from the mystery-cults of his day" is a "dead end" in New Testament studies (1987a:396).

The problems inherent to some of these older works on Christianity and the mysteries is assessed in *Bruce M. Metzger's* article "Methodology in the Study of the Mystery Religions and Early Christianity" (1968). In a mere twenty-four pages Metzger highlights a number of important issues and advocates methodological caution when undertaking the comparison.[26] His methodological caveats are worth summarizing here, although anyone pursuing the question of the influence of the mysteries on early Christianity will do well to read Metzger's article.[27]

1. There is some evidence of the influence of the rites and practices of the mysteries on the post-Constantinian church. For example, many sites for the veneration of heroes, with attendant mysteries, were taken over for the worship of saints. The practice of incubation in a

church building for the cure of a disease was similar to the practices of incubation in the cult of Asclepius. However, one cannot simply assume that the same influence was exerted in the pre-Constantinian period.

2. One must recognize that the evidence for the mysteries is scanty at best. It often dates from the third to the fifth centuries C.E. and comes from diverse geographical locations. It cannot be assumed that these same beliefs and practices were extant at the time of early Christianity.

3. The composition of the Palestinian church of strict monotheistic Jews intolerant of syncretism would give the church a certain reticence about borrowing from pagan cults.

4. Palestine, the seat of the earliest Christian communities, has yielded the least amount of archaeological data regarding the mysteries.

5. The existence of some parallels is clear, but they do not necessarily indicate Christian dependence on the mysteries. In fact, the parallels need to be evaluated closely, as sometimes they are manufactured by the scholar (e.g., Loisy, above). Where they are genuine, they may simply be analogical, due to a similar environment, rather than genealogical. Even where they are genealogical, it may be the case that the mysteries were influenced by Christianity.

6. Despite the similarities, the differences in both language and ideas between Christianity and the mysteries suggests independence. For example, the use of many important words from the mysteries is missing in Christianity; Christianity is grounded in an historical person, not a mythological character; Christianity was not shrouded in secrecy, but was simple and open; the rites of baptism and eucharist were very different in their essential components from the rites of the mysteries; and Jesus' death and resurrection differs in substance from the dying and rising of the pagan deities.

Not all of Metzger's methodological considerations are to be weighed equally. For example, in section 3 Metzger assumes a Jewish aversion of syncretism which may not have been the case, at least not for all Jews. Some aspects of first-century Judaism reflect some adoption of Hellenistic practices, and some Jews at least seem to have felt comfortable participating in non-Jewish religious practices (see Borgen 1995). Moreover, many of Metzger's assumptions about Christianity in section 6 can be called into question. His assumption that similarity means genealogical connections, while true of authors in the past, need not necessarily be made; analogical comparisons may indeed prove useful. Overall, however, Metzger is correct to advocate proper caution when examining ancient phenomena; caution in scholarly research is always well advised.

Newer Advocates

In an article published in 1980 assessing scholarship regarding the influence of the mysteries on early Christianity, ***Devon H. Wiens*** writes that due to the "unconvincing nature" of linguistic "parallels" and the "lack of demonstrated contacts," "the tide has turned in favor of a Jewish-oriented Paul," and that "Pauline thought can better be explained on the basis of his Jewish backgrounds" (Wiens 1980:1263). This is certainly seen in the work of those investigating the synagogue background of Paul's churches (chapter 1). However, in the 1980s there was a resurgence of interest in Paul's affinities with the philosophical schools of his day (as we saw in chapter 2), and now in the 1990s there is growing interest in the voluntary associations. Wiens's proclamation may have been premature. In fact, there are still a few scholars who find in the mysteries a compelling explanation for Pauline church formation. However, these scholars tend to work with much more methodological rigor than in the past.[28]

The exception to this methodological rigor is ***Howard M. Teeple's*** 1992 book *How Did Christianity Really Begin?*, which represents in some ways a modern return to the older history-of-religions school. Teeple is concerned with showing that Christianity does not have any original content but drew all of its thought and practice from other religions, particularly Judaism and the mysteries. Following Bousset and Bultmann's (now discredited) sharp distinction between the Palestinian church and the Hellenistic church, Teeple suggests that Paul received his baptismal theology through the influence of the mysteries, particularly that of Mithras, which he then went on to modify in light of the death and resurrection of Jesus (1992:198–201). Overall, Teeple's book is unsuccessful. His assertions seem unfounded and his use of secondary sources is dated. Much better work has been done of late regarding Paul's relationship to the mysteries.

One such work is that of **Hyam Maccoby**—*Paul and Hellenism* (1991). He completely rejects claims that Paul's doctrine of salvation can be derived from Jewish sources, either directly or as a logical development.[29] Instead, he suggests that Paul was influenced by Gnosticism and, more importantly, the mysteries. Maccoby summarizes Paul's doctrine of salvation as containing six elements (1991:55):

(1) the hopeless moral condition of humankind;
(2) the descent of the divine savior in a human body;
(3) the violent death of the divine savior;
(4) resurrection, immortality and divinity of the crucified savior;
(5) vicarious atonement effected by the divine death for those who have faith in its efficacy;
(6) promise of resurrection and immortality to devotees of the savior.

Maccoby investigates each element individually and in order. He begins by showing that efforts to ground Paul's view of the human condition in the Judaism of his time have all proven to be unsuccessful. The same holds true regarding the idea of the descent of a divine savior. There is in the Hellenistic world, particularly Gnosticism, such a figure, which Maccoby hints is the source for Paul. Paul's view of the *violent* death of the divine savior has no analogue in Judaism or Gnosticism. According to Maccoby, "a satisfactory analogue can be found only in the mystery religions" where the violent death of a savior deity is found often (1991:65). This Maccoby illustrates from various figures of the mysteries such as Dionysus, Sarapis, Adonis, Attis and Orpheus. All of these figures, he suggests, have some pre-death characteristics of divinity and are to be seen as gods. Paul is the one who attributes this aspect of the mysteries to Jesus, thus merging Gnosticism and the mysteries.

The concepts of resurrection, immortality and the divinity of a person all find their origin in the mysteries—the "dying-and-rising gods" such as Dionysus, Adonis, Baal and Sarapis. These concepts come to Paul exclusively through the mysteries, since they are antithetical to Gnostic ideas on the corporeality of the body. The idea that atonement is effected by the divine death is also based not in Judaism but in the mysteries. While the idea of atonement can be found in

Judaism, it is not brought about through a willing human sacrifice whose death averts the wrath of the god and purges the devotees of their sins (1991:78). Finally, the concept of resurrection and immortality came to Paul through Gnosticism and the mysteries, although Maccoby also suggests the influence of the latter on Gnosticism as well (1991:83). Thus, Paul's central soteriological concern came as a direct influence of the mysteries and, secondarily, Gnosticism. Judaism had no part to play in the process.[30]

In the next chapter Maccoby pushes his thesis further by arguing that the eucharist originated with Paul and, as such, has most affinities "not with the Jewish *qiddush* but with the ritual meals of the mystery religions" (1991:90). Much study has been devoted to the origin of the eucharist by New Testament scholars, so Maccoby spends a number of pages (90–122) disputing the evidence that ties the eucharist to the Jewish world. Four aspects of the eucharist according to Paul (1 Cor 11:23–26) stand out as being most like the communion meals of the mysteries. The name "the Lord's supper" (*kyriakon deipnon*) used by Paul for the rite, is like the expression used in other cults where the central salvific figure is addressed and designated as "Lord." Paul's emphasis on the bread (by inverting the wine-bread order of the Jewish meal) is similar to the mysteries which focus on food as indicative of the fertility of the land in producing crops (e.g., the Eleusinian mysteries in which an ear of corn is central). In using the expression "after supper," Paul might be tying the wine to the pagan practice of celebrating the pre-Olympic deity *agathos daimon,* who lies behind several deities of the mysteries (1991:124). Finally, and most importantly according to Maccoby, the idea that the partaker is actually eating the body and blood of the deity when partaking of bread and wine is based on the mysteries rather than Judaism (in which it was forbidden to eat blood). In so doing, the believer is thought to be entering mystic community with the deity and sharing in his immortality.

In a brief postscript Maccoby suggests that the best analogue for Pauline baptism is not Jewish ideas of purification, but the once-for-all rites of initiation in the mysteries. Maccoby's work can best be described as controversial, and his conclusions have not been widely accepted.

In an earlier study ***Hans Dieter Betz*** (1968) pointed out a number

of comparisons between Mithraic inscriptions from the Mithras sanctuary found under the Church of Santa Prisca in Rome and the New
Testament. Although the inscriptions are later than the New Testament
texts, Betz suggests that as cultic material they go back to older traditions and must therefore be earlier than or contemporary with first-century Christianity. Betz is not interested in showing a direct dependency
of one religious group upon the other; rather, "[a] comparison of the
forms and concepts, however, will lead us to a better understanding of
the structures of Hellenistic mystery cult ideas on both sides, the
Mithras religion as well as the early Christian" (1968:64).

Although the Mithraic inscriptions are in Latin, the ideas expressed in them have similarities with much of Paul's language.[31] For
example, the incantation of the elements of the world found in line 1—
"Fertile earth Pales who procreates everything"—finds affinity with the
polemic against worshipping the elements of the world in Galatians 4:8
(as well as Colossians and Revelation). Paul's polemic indicates that
within Christian groups it was at least conceivable that some members
would worship the elements of the world. The hymnic reference in line
4 of the inscriptions to a spring coming forth from a rock when impacted by Mithras' arrow is similar to Paul's discussion in 1 Corinthians 10
of Christ the Rock that supplied the Israelites with water in the desert.
Although the immediate referent for this is the Old Testament and a
Hellenistic-Jewish Midrash on it (cf. Philo), it is clear that Paul has
"interpreted the Midrash in a way which is typical of mystery cult
ideas" (1968:67).

The poetic reference in line 7 to Mithras carrying the bull on his
shoulders (toward the cave in which the bull would be slain) sounds
similar to paraenetical interpretations of carrying the "death of Jesus" (2
Cor 4:10; Gal 6:17) or the burdens of others or of oneself (Rom 15:1;
Gal 6:2, 5). Concern for the cares of this world found in line 10 resonate
with such concern in Paul's letters. Line 11 makes reference to a person
"piously reborn," much like Paul's reference to the Christian as a new
creation (1 Cor 5:17; Gal 6:15). Exhortation to endure difficult times
together are found in line 12 of the inscriptions and throughout the
Pauline corpus. The confessional formula of line 14, "and you saved us
after having shed the eternal blood" sounds strikingly like early
Christian confessions such as Romans 3:25.

All of these indicate affinities between the Mithraic mysteries and

Pauline Christianity. While Betz does not tie this directly to community formation, he hints at it, noting that the exhortations in both sets of data are aimed at the community of believers rather than individuals. However, he does note that the "universalism" of early Christian ecclesiology[32] sets it apart from the self-understanding of the Mithras cult (1968:74; cf. Nock 1972b, esp. 458).

In a much later work Betz (1995) turns his attention to Paul's view of baptism as presented in Romans 6. Again, he suggests that Paul's understanding has affinities with the mysteries. However, this time he makes the connection more directly. Paul's view of baptism, Betz suggests, came originally through the Palestinian environment, in particular, the influence of John the Baptist in the early church. Paul cites an earlier baptismal formula in Galatians 3:26–28, but develops it differently when writing 1 Corinthians. However, his most complete reflection on baptism, found in Romans 6:3–10, "sets forth a new kind of baptismal theology" (1995:86) based on, but substantially developed from, Galatians 3:26–28 (1995:107–8).

As the founder figure of the Gentile Christian groups,[33] Paul was one of the primary figures responsible for introducing substantial changes into "the traditions, rituals, and organization of Palestinian Christianity" (1995:100). Thus, in Romans 6 Paul interprets baptism as the Christian initiation ritual, which functions much like the initiation rituals found in many of the Hellenistic mysteries. In this regard, Paul was influenced by the mysteries.

In light of the critiques of the mysteries as an analogy for Pauline Christian communities, some scholars opt for arguing for more limited contact between the mysteries and Pauline Christianity. For example, **Karl P. Donfried** (1985) looks at Thessalonica and argues that recognition of the civic and religious history of the city must be the essential starting point for understanding both the earliest Christian community there and Paul's first letter to them (1985:336–56).[34]

To that end, Donfried surveys the deities popular in Thessalonica during the first century C.E.: Sarapis, Dionysus, Cabirus and the Emperor. Throughout the article he shows how Paul has carefully chosen his terminology when writing the letter so that it would serve "protreptic purposes" (1985:353). That is to say, it would have resonated well with the terminology of the mystery cults and the royal theology that filled the Thessalonians' city, not to mention figured largely in their past. However, Paul uses such language not to turn Christianity into a mystery cult, but to show how completely the Thessalonians' lives have been altered in their "new living relationship" with Christ (1985:353). Nevertheless, the local manifestations of Thessalonica determine how Paul will help form the Christian community's self-identity.

In a much more thorough study of *The Thessalonian Correspondence* (1986), **Robert Jewett** also focuses on Paul's community at Thessalonica. In this investigation of 1 and 2 Thessalonians, Jewett uses both rhetorical analysis and information from the political, economic, social and religious context of Thessalonica to reconstruct the community situation. He concludes that Paul's letters address a situation of "millenarian radicalism" (1986:xiii) that caused members of the Thessalonian congregation to proclaim the actual arrival of the millennium and to act accordingly. The deflation of this millenarian faith by the onset of persecution and the death of members of the congregation gave Paul cause to write his first letter. However, in addressing this crisis, Paul caused some radicals to regenerate their excitement to the point of antinomian behavior and the declaration that the Day of the Lord had arrived. In order to bring this situation under control, Paul sent 2 Thessalonians.

Jewett suggests that the Cabirus mystery cult was influential on the development of the Thessalonian church. The figure of Cabirus was similar to that of Christ: both suffered a martyr's death and both were expected to return physically. The cult of Cabirus was the most important religious cult in Thessalonica during Paul's time there. Although it had originally been very popular among the lower classes, at the time of Paul it was solidly in the purview of the civic magistrates. This left the poorer workers very receptive to Christ (1986:165). These workers became the millenarian radicals, refusing to work, living sexually licentious lives and refusing to acknowledge the community leaders, all in preparation for the Parousia, which they were already experiencing in ecstatic activities. When Paul fails to fulfill the expected role of the priest of Cabirus, the radicals deride him before the congregation. Paul addresses this group as the *ataktoi,* the "rebellious," and attempts to reign them in and to reestablish the proper mode of behavior appropriate to an apocalyptic future.

Jewett's work has received positive reviews, although his conjecture that the Cabirus cult influenced the development of Christianity at Thessalonica has been cited as needing more support.[35] Despite his attempts to control preconceived assumptions about the Thessalonian Christians through the use of rhetorical criticism (1986:xiv), Jewett cannot escape allowing selective analyses and unwarranted assumptions to creep into his work.[36]

Conclusion

Overall, it is clear that the mysteries have not proven very helpful on a large scale for understanding early Christianity. The general failure of the history-of-religions school to convince scholars of mystery influences has led to their being considered unimportant.[37] However, more recent studies that have looked at individual aspects of individual mysteries and/or have tied their studies to the religious life in specific locales have proven more fruitful. Here, the concepts of the mysteries illuminate some aspects of Pauline thought and Christian community formation in a way that the sweeping claims of the history-of-religions school never did.

Even more helpful is **Gary Lease** (1980), who strikes a balance between those who see the mysteries exerting a significant influence on Pauline Christianity and those who deny any influence. Lease points out that due to the shared world of the mysteries and formative Christianity, "the question of direct and conscious mutual influence and borrowings between Christianity and other late-antiquity religions becomes an extremely complicated and perhaps insoluble question" (1980:1315). He goes on to outline some of the similarities between Mithraism and Christianity in the areas of doctrine (cosmogony, redeeming mediator, eschatology); origins (redeemer's birth, the cave, celebration); and ritual practice (baptism, cultic meal, purification, holy war).[38] In all these cases he admits it is difficult to identify elements of derivation or direct influence; "neither Mithraism nor Christianity proved to be an obvious and direct influence upon the other in the development and demise or survival of either religion" (1980:1329).

In reaching this conclusion Lease points to the shared cultural background of Mithraism and Christianity. Once Christianity left

Palestine, it encountered the "broader non-Jewish Hellenistic world of late antiquity" (1980:1328). Here it was competing with other religions, including Mithraism, for the adherence of people who were seeking a different religious experience than that of their ancestors. Their world had changed, and with it so had their religious aspirations. In those tumultuous times many were seeking a release from the overwhelming burden of fate and its control over human existence. For many, this "led to an emphasis upon the personal, ritual confrontation with the transcendent" (1980:1309).

It should not be surprising to find various competing religious movements addressing these and other concerns with similar language, beliefs and practices. Some mutual influence, consciously or not, is almost impossible to avoid. We will return to the implications of this observation in our conclusion; for now we simply note that it opens up the way for a much broader understanding of early Christianity by high-lighting which needs of the people these competing groups were addressing and how they were doing so. Such an investigation would lead to a much more nuanced understanding of early Christianity, even if no progress was made on the "sources" of certain ideas and practices.

4
Voluntary Associations

Paul and the Voluntary Associations

In Acts 19:9 Luke refers to Paul, upon having left the synagogue at Ephesus, teaching in the *scholē* of Tyrannus. While this is usually thought to be a lecture hall, and thus evidence for Paul being a wandering philosopher, **Abraham J. Malherbe** observes that the word is also a common designation for a guild hall (Malherbe 1983:90). Such guild halls were also frequently named after the patron of the guild. Thus, Luke might be presenting a picture of the early church at Ephesus as a guild which meets in the *scholē* of Tyrannus. While in Ephesus Paul not only teaches but also works at his trade, that of tentmaking, suggesting frequent contact with workers who could have formed the core of the Ephesian church (Malherbe 1983:90–91).

In a short study entitled "Our *Politeuma* is in Heaven: The Meaning of Philippians 3:17–21" (1993), **Wendy Cotter** argues that the voluntary associations provide the interpretive backdrop for Paul's warning to the Philippians. Voluntary associations were often repudiated for their overindulgence in food and drink and sexual excess, and would clearly fit Paul's description "their god is the belly, and they glory in their shame, with minds set on earthly things" (Phil 3:19). It is such a way of life that must not be copied by the Philippian Christians. Paul contrasts the Philippians' life with that of these "opponents" by suggesting that "our *politeuma* is in heaven." In using this phrase, Cotter suggests, Paul has picked up the vocabulary of his opponents and used it to reaffirm the Philippians' calling to a greater honor in the future. The references to the practices of the associations, along with the use of the word *politeuma,* and its verbal form *politeuesthai* in Philippians 1:27, and references to leaders using titles taken from the offices of both the city and the associations (*episkopoi* and *diakonoi,* Phil 1:1), indicate that the community model used by the Philippian church was that of the voluntary associations. Paul writes to them as he does in order to warn them that despite using the associations as a community model, they are not to adopt "the attending ambitious and worldly behavior typical of political and civic organizations" (1993:104).

In 1981 *S. C. Barton* and *G. H. R. Horsley* published a lengthy analysis entitled "A Hellenistic Cult Group and the New Testament Churches," in which they study an inscription from Philadelphia (*SIG*[3] 985), which details the regulations of a private voluntary association. In their analysis they point out some similarities that early Christianity, particularly Pauline Christianity, shared with cult groups (particularly that of Philadelphia). In terms of origins, both types of groups were comprised of "voluntary" membership, and both relied on private initiative in their founding. Both also relied on cooperation and hospitality, particularly the opening of houses for religious gatherings. Both also offered security and salvation in an age of uncertainty about traditional institutions. The role of the deity is similar in each group. In the Philadelphia inscription the god Zeus appears to the founder of the club, Dionysius, and imparts the club ordinances to him. Likewise, the New Testament is full of references to God speaking to people through dreams and prophecies, particularly with reference to the expansion of the new movement across the empire (for example, Acts 9:1–19; 10:1–48; 16:9; Gal 2:2; 2 Cor 12:1–4). In both groups the deity advocates moral purity among the adherents and threatens divine sanction if it is not attained. Both groups met in private places of meeting, commonly referred to as an *oikos,* which usually belonged to a member of the community (see 1 Cor 16:19; Rom 16:5; Phlm 2; Col 4:15). Both groups held regular meetings and had special days for celebration each year.

One of the most important topics of comparison is that of membership. Both groups were open to persons of either gender and neither took social class into account. In fact, the involvement of women (and slaves) in the associations, to a degree not found in public institutions, "set a precedent for the Christians to emulate" (1981:33). Both groups also had a strong moral code as a condition for membership (the associations as a condition and the Christians as a result), particularly in the area of sexual ethics and social vices (that which pertains to group rather than personal life, e.g., hospitality). Failure to meet the standard set by the group resulted in a loss of membership, and thus, expulsion from the group. Within both groups there was a marked absence of differentiation on the basis of hierarchy, with both groups being "egalitarian and participatory" (1981:38).

In terms of practice, the only significant analogy that Barton and Horsley find between the two groups is the voluntary gathering together for a religious purpose in a private house (*oikos*). The activities undertaken therein are much different (see below). In terms of aims, both groups were concerned with morality over ritual. However, Christianity, for Barton and Horsley, comes closer to the philosophical schools than does the Philadelphian association, to the extent to which they suggest that the Christians groups were a combination of a cult association and a philosophical school (cf. Wilken 1971). Finally, the association and the Christian groups emphasized the communal aspects of community life over those of individualism.

A number of important differences are pointed out by Barton and Horsley. First, the cult groups tended to be localized while Christianity was more international in scope (1981:28). While they do note (1981:28) that the local character of the Christian groups was much like that of localized cult groups, they emphasize Christianity's worldwide connections. Second, the deity, while present in both groups, was not represented physically in the Christian groups as it was in the association, giving the Christian groups an unusual "noncultic" character (1981:30). Third, morality for the association was a prerequisite (or "condition") for entrance into the cult, while in the Christian groups, moral purity followed upon a commitment of faith in Jesus the resurrected Lord (thus, it was a "sign"; 1981:30–31). Fourth, Christian meetings were more frequent than that of the Philadelphia association, occurring daily or weekly rather than monthly. As well, the "active proselytising" of the Christian groups set them apart from the "voluntary associations" (1981:34).

Despite the similarities in the moral codes of the two groups the

Christian groups were more rigorous in their moral injunctions, focusing not only on the suppression of vices but also on the exhibition of virtues (1981:37). Along with this went a certain elevation of some spiritual gifts over others, thus resulting in more respect accorded some people over others, somewhat belying the intended egalitarian nature of the Christian communities. The eighth difference between the two groups was the early Christians' lack of iconography, mysteries, purifications and expiations, and sacrifices. Instead, their meetings included prayers, hymns, teaching and the sharing of a common meal. In many ways membership in the Christian group was much more open to outsiders and the uninitiated (1981:39). Finally, the cult association at Philadelphia sought salvation from Zeus in this world, while the Christian groups looked for salvation in the world to come.

Barton and Horsley do make it clear that the purpose of the comparison of Christian churches and voluntary associations is to draw analogies between the two, suggesting that insufficient evidence exists to demonstrate direct influence (1981:7). Despite the differences between the two groups to which they point, the voluntary associations are an important analogy for ancient Christian groups, and one worth pursuing. In fact, they suggest that "Paul's idea of community would have been attractive to members of private cult-groups analogous to that at Philadelphia" (1981:39), indicating that Pauline churches might have been formed from such people.

Nature and Extent of Voluntary Associations

Description[1]

A voluntary association might be generally defined as "a group which a man [or woman] joins of his own free will, and which accepts him of its free will, and this mutual acceptance creates certain obligations on both parties" (Roberts, Skeat, Nock 1936:75; cf. Meeks 1983:78). It is "a coherent group, which could be recognized as such by outsiders, with its own rules for membership, leadership and association with one another" (Gaston 1993:85). Such associations existed from as early as the fifth or fourth century B.C.E. until well into the Roman imperial period. In the Hellenistic period the voluntary associations began to grow in importance, and by the time of the Roman empire they are attested in almost every city and town, despite official attempts to suppress them.

Our primary source of information about voluntary associations comes from inscriptions. The associations' membership, decrees and statutes were engraved upon stone and set up for public reading (cf. Schmeller 1995:24). Such inscriptions, unlike papyri, have weathered fairly well throughout the former Roman Empire.[2]

A number of terms were used in antiquity for voluntary associations, originally with differing meanings, although these nuances began to fade over time: *orgeōnes, thiasos* and *eranos* (see Danker 1992:501; cf. Tod 1932:74–75). Roman associations were generally termed *collegia.* Other Greek terms used for associations or their members include *ephēboi, neoi* (or *neōteroi*), *ekklēsia, synagōguē, synodos, koinon,* and in Latin, *sodalitas* and *fratres.*

Due to this range of terms used and compounded by the type of evidence available, it is difficult to clearly distinguish the various types of associations (Kloppenborg 1996a:18). Three broad categories of associations are usually distinguished (Kloppenborg 1996a:18). Funerary associations were organized to insure the proper burial of their deceased members. In exchange, members paid entrance fees and/or regular dues that would be pooled for the burials. Although associations which ostensibly were formed solely for the burial of members did not exist until the second century C.E., many associations did undertake the proper burial of their members even before this time (Kloppenborg 1996a:21). Often, such funerary associations also functioned as social clubs, with members meeting regularly for banquets. Another offshoot of the funerary association were those associations founded or endowed by a patron for the purpose of commemorating the anniversary of his or her death at the family tomb.

Religious associations were dedicated to the worship of a particular deity or deities through cultic acts and special festival days. Such associations might also include a public procession. Some associations performed public functions in connection with worship, usually in public temples, while others were private associations which gathered most often in private shrines (Roberts, Skeat, Nock 1936:75).

Professional associations formed by traders or specialized workers are attested in both the Hellenistic (Fisher 1988a:1195) and the Roman periods (Jones 1955, esp. 170–86). Large associations of foreign merchants and artisans were formed in almost all of the cities of the empire, especially in the larger commercial centers (e.g., Rome, Corinth, Ephesus; Meeks 1983:32). Since most artisans would live and work in one particular area of a city, it would be easy for them to form themselves into associations (Kloppenborg 1996a:24). Professional associations of Dionysiac artists also flourished throughout the Roman Empire.

Although these three general categories of funerary, religious and professional are helpful, there was much crossing over, and many associations functioned in a number of different ways. Thus, professional trade association might also be dedicated to the worship of a particular deity and undertake the burial of its members.

The primary function of voluntary associations was religious and social. Almost all of the voluntary associations were concerned with the worship of a deity and claimed its protection. Most met together for common meals, either on an entirely social basis or in connection with a sacrifice to the god(s) or a commemoration at the tomb of a deceased member or patron. Except in a very few instances, even the trade associations banded together for mutual worship and fellowship rather than for the betterment of working conditions or increased pay (see further Kloppenborg 1996a:19–20).

Voluntary associations were relatively small groups. Only rarely did an association have more than one hundred members, although evidence exists for associations of up to three to four hundred members (McLean 1993:257), and even an association of twelve hundred members (Kloppenborg 1996a:30, n. 64). It would also be unusual for an association to have fewer than ten members. Usually, associations had a membership of between twenty and fifty persons (cf. Schmeller 1995:40).

Most associations "were composed of the urban poor, slaves, and freedmen" (Kloppenborg 1996a:23), although some members clearly came from the upper ranks of society. Women are attested as equal members in some associations, although the membership of professional associations was more likely to be divided according to gender, with all male professional associations connected with those professions dominated by men and all female associations related to professions dominated by women (see Whelan 1993:75–76 and nn. 20–23; Kloppenborg 1996a:25).

Patrons played an important role in voluntary associations.[3] In exchange for large financial donations which allowed them to exist and to hold banquets and festivals, voluntary associations publicly honored their benefactors. The patron of an association could be a man or a woman, at times even an entire family.[4] Often a single association could have several patrons, or a single patron could benefact several associations at once (Schmeller 1995:33).

Schmeller (1995:35) suggests that patrons were simply "honorary presidents" and not actually members of the association; they did not participate in the assemblies, exercised no direct control of the group and did not place any restrictions on the use of the money. However, a number of inscriptions argue against this point, suggesting that often (although not always) a patron did function as president and was active at meetings. A patron could also determine how funds were to be disbursed (particularly in testamentary foundations) and could even appoint some of the officials (often from members of his or her extended family).

Officials were common in the associations, and there was a "positive exuberance" with granting titles to functionaries (Meeks 1983:134). Often these officials imitated both the titles and functions of civic officials (Meeks 1983:31, 134). Officials were responsible for the sacrifices, banquets and festivals (priests; priestesses), the collection and dispersment of monies (treasurers), and the convening and chairing of meetings (presidents). A person might be elected to one of these positions by the members of the association or in some cases the office would be purchased by the highest bidder. Either way, serving in such a capacity often could bring with it a heavy financial burden, as the official was required to expend his or her own money in carrying out the requisite duties. In exchange, of course, he or she received multiple honors (statues, crowns, proclamations, inscriptions) from the association members.

Within many associations there was both hierarchy and equality (cf. Schmeller 1995:42). The hierarchy existed between the founder and the officials of the association, many of whom received larger portions of the meat from the sacrifices than did the general membership.

However, among the members themselves it is common to find citizens and noncitizens, masters and slaves, men and women, and rich and poor, all fellowshipping together in one association. Professional/trade associations would be the most socially homogeneous (Schmeller 1995:49); other types of associations were less so.

There were a number of personal benefits of belonging to an association. Membership in an association gave a person a sense of belonging in an age where many were dislodged from the traditional security of family, friends and homeland (primarily through either military service or trade; Kloppenborg 1996a:17–18). Life could be more enjoyable through membership in an association. Many associations also provided a network of social support within the larger society. Some groups even contributed funds to members who fell on hard times (cf. Renan 1866:281). However, there is little evidence of associations contributing to the needs of the poor who were not members (Danker 1992:502). There is the obvious benefit of the guarantee of a decent burial with the possibility of the annual commemoration of one's death. Finally, participation in an association allowed for the attainment of honor, prestige and authority through the replication of the organizational structure of the city (*polis*). A person could thus reach a status "to which he or she could never aspire outside of the association" (Kloppenborg 1996a:18).

Propagation[5]

There is evidence for a number of methods of forming and propagating voluntary association throughout antiquity. Here we will simply highlight a few of the procedures whereby an association was formed, procedures which were subsequently referred to in inscriptions. These incorporate actions taken by individuals (including testamentary foundations), merchants and the gods (dreams and visions, oracles).

Private voluntary associations could be formed by individuals for a number of purposes, although the primary reasons seem to have been performance of cultic rites, particularly funerary rites, and gathering for social interchange. Generally one person would invite others to form an association, or a number of persons would collectively decide to do so (Liebenam 1890:169; Waltzing 1895:337). Such associations were often named after their founders.

Local private associations could also be formed from larger cultic associations such as that of Sarapis and Isis. An inscription from Thessalonica records how the cult was brought to a small town and established in the home of a woman who became the first priestess. Eventually the association was opened up to a wider group of adherents (see *IG* X/2 255). As in this case, the patron divinity of an association was often involved in the foundation, growth and development of voluntary associations, particularly through the use of dreams, visions and oracles. Often an individual would make a legal will establishing an endowment which would be given to a particular association to enact rites in memory of the deceased. In some cases, an already existing association was endowed, but very often a new association was to be formed.

Associations concerned with a particular trade could be formed in a particular locale when enough people of that trade lived in the area. Another commonality which led to the formation of an association was ethnic background; people of similar origins would form associations to provide mutual support and a context for various socioreligious events to take place.

It is clear from the evidence that there were a number of ways and a number of reasons that voluntary associations could be formed in antiquity. Once formed, they attracted members, often outgrowing their original meeting places. We do not have evidence for a strong missionizing tendency in any of the associations, but it is clear from the study of a number of associations that they attracted new members and sometimes established new groups, both in their home areas and in other locales.

Voluntary Associations as a Model

The use of voluntary associations as an analogy for early Christian groups is "by no means a new thought" (Countryman 1977:135). As early as the second and third centuries, both Christians and non-Christians were comparing Christian groups to the voluntary associations (Schmeller 1995:10; Wilken 1971; 1984 [summarized below]). Many scholars in the late nineteenth and early twentieth century often assumed that the earliest Christian groupings were voluntary associations.

Two of the earliest scholars to actually argue that the Christian groups were collegia were **Theodor Mommsen** and **Giovanni de Rossi.**[6] Mommsen's study, *De collegiis et sodaliciis Romanorum* (1843 [*Concerning Roman Associations and Sodalities*]), laid the foundation for most subsequent study of the subject. He was one of the first to show that Christian groups have the characteristics of a voluntary association. Prior to Mommsen, studies had only pointed to isolated inscriptions, especially in the debates over the legal position of the associations. In his *La Roma sotteranea cristiana* (1864–77 [*The Roman Christian Catacombs*]) de Rossi, an archaeologist, investigates Christian cemeteries and concludes from the evidence that the Christian communities were recognized burial societies.

In 1866 **Ernest Renan** published *The Apostles,*[7] in which he includes a chapter on the voluntary associations (1866:278–89). His primary interest is the restrictions placed on the associations by various emperors. Although he does not argue for a direct connection between the two types of groups, he does suggest that both provided similar benefits to their members, and that the Christian groups would have fallen under the same suspicion as the associations by those in authority (prefects and governors).

In 1876 **Georg Heinrici,** in "Die Christengemeinden Korinths und die religiösen Genossenschaften der Griechen" ("The Christian Community of Corinth and the Greek Religious Associations"), compared the Corinthian church with voluntary associations, something he continued to maintain in publications over the next twenty years (1877; 1881; 1896). A number of factors convinced Heinrici that the association provided a better model than the synagogues for understanding the early Christian groups (Kloppenborg 1993a:215). He points to the common use of the name *ekklēsia* for the group, the use of other terms from associations to describe the Christian groups, their common religious character, their open membership that included both men and women, their support of the poor, the use of the body metaphor to describe their community and the use of familial terms in referring to members. This leads him to conclude that the Corinthian community organized itself like a voluntary association (for a summary see Schmeller 1995:11–13).

Another important early scholar was **Edwin Hatch** (1881, esp.

26–39 and 1891:283–309).[8] Hatch was a great Greek scholar, and he was able to make good use of the plethora of Greek inscriptions which were becoming readily available through the publication of various corpora. He argues that all of the elements of the early church organization can be traced to Greco-Roman institutions, particularly the associations (Hatch 1881:208–9; cf. 1881:36).[9] In his second Bampton lecture, Hatch notes a number of similarities between Christian groups and the associations: "they had the same names for their meetings and some of the same names for their officers," the members of each group professed a common religion, the members of each "contributed to or received from a common fund," they shared a common meal, admission was open and included not only freeborn citizens but also women, strangers, freedmen and slaves (1881:30–31). The primary difference between the two groups was in their charity. While the associations were charitable to their own members as a matter of course, the Christian groups were deliberate in their pursuit of providing relief to the poor (1881:35–36).

Almost a decade later, Hatch would pursue this thought in another series of lectures. Here he points out that the voluntary associations and Christianity shared the same aims: "the aim of worshipping a pure God, the aim of living a pure life, and the aim of cultivating the spirit of brotherhood" (1891:292); and the same sanction: "the fear of *future punishments*" (1891:292, n. 2, his emphasis). Moreover, Hatch suggests that since Christianity drew some of its members from other associations, it would inevitably assimilate "some of the elements of these existing groups," although this happened after the apostolic age (Hatch 1891:292–93).

In the tenth chapter of his 1906 book *Studies in Roman History,* **E. G. Hardy** suggests that Christianity was very similar to associations (1906:129–50). In fact, he asserts that the Christian communities would have resembled the associations and been numbered among them by outsiders (1906:131, 141). Despite an edict of Augustus limiting the existence of voluntary associations, a great number of varying sorts continued to proliferate throughout the empire, most without the required special permission. It is among these unlicensed associations that Christianity best fits. Much of the early part of the chapter is taken up with a discussion over the legal status of the unofficial associations and the attitude of the governing authorities towards them.

Having determined that the Christian associations could well have existed and grown, with the occasional conflict with authorities, Hardy then investigates the nature of Christian groups as associations. Similarities to the pagan associations include the diversity of terms used to describe the groups. However, Christianity does have some differing features which may have caused them to be investigated by the authorities, features such as successive growth and daily common meals that raised suspicions about them as *hetaeriae,* politically disruptive clubs (1906:142). Nevertheless, for Hardy, the voluntary associations of antiquity are the best analogy for understanding early Christian groups.

In his discussion of "illegal and unofficial collegia" in *The Legislation of the Greeks and Romans on Corporations* (1910) **Max Radin** includes a brief section on the Christian churches (1910:126–28). Radin makes it clear that Christian groups were the same as voluntary associations. In fact, he suggests that "worship" was unthinkable in any other form at that time (1910:127). In terms of legal status, Christianity was tolerated in the same way as the majority of other associations, including "the privileged Jewish ones" (1910:128). Local magistrates used their discretion in deciding whether to prosecute individuals who were involved in such associations.

Thomas Wilson devotes a chapter of his book *St. Paul and Paganism* (1927) to a study of "St. Paul and the Pagan Guilds" (1927:120–35). He begins with a brief, readable survey of the associations, focusing his attention on the varieties of associations based on their names. He then suggests that the number of Gentile converts to Christianity in Paul's churches would lead congregations to lean more naturally toward the model of the guild system rather than the synagogue for their internal structure and corporate life (1927:124). Neither the associations nor the churches possessed legal recognition by the authorities, but both managed to survive any attempts at suppression. In terms of numbers, both groups were kept relatively small, being somewhere between thirty and two hundred members.[10] Terminology within both groups was similar, particularly in the use of *ekklēsia* and "presbyter." Both were religious associations specifically linked to some cult,[11] and both had a strong sense of communion with the patron deity.[12] In particular, a focus on the sacred drama of the deity was important. In the case of Christianity this was the passion, death, resurrection and exaltation of Jesus.

The Pauline concept of Christian kinship relations and heavenly citizenry also finds an analogy in the associations. Both groups met in houses belonging to members in order to partake of some special type of meal together. This developed into a special house for the guilds and church buildings for the Christians. Along with this meal went a spirit of sharing of possessions manifested in both the Christian groups and the associations. This arose out of their shared sense of equality, particularly in terms of class distinctions and gender. In fact, there was a sense of freedom of speech in the churches and the associations that was not found elsewhere. Finally, the guilds and the churches both placed a heavy emphasis on one's duty to work and the avoidance of idleness as well as on one's moral duty to one's fellow human beings. Wilson concludes by affirming that the guilds contributed greatly to the character of the Christian communities and were as much a part of the providential preparation for the coming of Christianity as Judaism and the Old Testament.

In the introduction we noted that *E. A. Judge* sees the voluntary associations as an institution that proved attractive to many people in the Roman Empire. In his *The Social Pattern of Christian Groups in the First Century* (1960b), he discusses the voluntary associations under the rubric of "unofficial associations" or "koinōnia." After surveying briefly the characteristics of the voluntary associations, he suggests that there existed both Jewish and Christian associations in the first century.[13] Such associations were "unincorporated rather than illegal" (1960b:43), that is, they were unrecognized officially. Judge points out that there are a few differences between the Christian groups and the associations. First, he suggests that Christians had "international links" like the Jews, although he admits that, unlike the Jews, they lacked a national seat for their cult. However, he goes on to suggest that, while unusual, the international links "do not seriously qualify the similarity at the local level" (1960b:46). Second, he suggests that Christian associations drew from a much broader constituency (from rich to slave) than other associations.[14]

Despite these differences, Judge concludes that, in the mind of the public, Christians would not have been distinguished from other unofficial associations (1960b:44).[15] And Christians themselves would not have questioned that they were forming voluntary associations of the usual kind (1960b:45). In fact, the description of the early Jerusalem community in the opening chapters of Acts could easily serve as a description of the activities of other associations: "initiation, the mysteries, equal partnership, ceremonial meal, the cult, wonder-working, mutual benefits" (1960b:47). By the second century, despite many problems of factionalism along the way (reflected in 1 Corinthians), Christian groups were still being understood as voluntary associations (see Pliny, *Epistulae* 10.96).

In the latter part of the book Judge investigates the social constituency of the Christian groups. He points out that while it is true that Christian groups were not constituted from the upper orders of society, this would also be true for other local cult associations (1960b:52). In general, most people, Christian or otherwise, did not meet members of the Roman aristocracy (1960b:54). Yet, within the Christian groups there was a diversity of people from various other social strata represented, both within local groups and among groups from other locales. Christian groups were dominated by those higher in the social order, although they drew on a broad constituency of the population, especially insofar as they incorporated entire households into the fold (1960b:60–61).

In the early 1970s **Robert Wilken** published an essay entitled "Christianity, Philosophical Schools, and Collegia" (1971) in which he investigates how Christianity appeared to men and women of the Greco-Roman world. This was followed in 1984 with a book-length treatment of the same subject. Wilken's primary objective in his article is to investigate what conceptions were available to the outsider who observed the Christian movement.[16] Two social movements are used as an analogy for early Christianity: burial societies and philosophical schools (for a summary of his position on the latter see chapter 2).

After describing briefly the character of the voluntary associations in antiquity, Wilken turns to the letters of Pliny to show that the Christians were understood as an association much like the other associations in the area of Bythinia (*Epistulae* 10.96). Some time later Celsus charged the Christians with existing illegally, since they met in secret, and secret societies were illegal (Origen, *Contra Celsum* 1.1; 8.17, 47). Other hints of such an understanding of Christianity are found in the writings of Alexander Severus (*Historia Augusta, Vita Alex.* 49), who describes an altercation over a meeting place that arose between an association of cooks and an association of Christians. Tertullian

(*Apologia* 38–39) provides the most significant evidence. He argues that Christianity should be reckoned among the legal associations, since they were not a political club but a harmless association like so many that were found in cities and towns. Tertullian's description is full of terms more descriptive of associations than the theological language often used for Christian churches (Wilken 1971:283).

Despite the ancient descriptions of Christianity as an association, Wilken finds an important difference. The voluntary associations were exclusively local groups while Christianity was "a 'worldwide' sect whose adherents lived throughout the Mediterranean world and shared a common religious profession and style of life" (Wilken 1971:287). This is more like the philosophical schools than the voluntary associations which "were not 'international,'" that is, "a group of associations bound together in an organization extending across the Mediterranean world" (Wilken 1984:35). Ultimately, Christianity, for Wilken, is more like the Stoics or Epicureans, in reaching beyond local boundaries. He does, however, concede that on the local level Christianity "engaged in much the same activities as other associations" (Wilken 1971:287). For Wilken, while philosophical schools were not the same as associations, often a number of shared features between the two types of groups can be found: terminology, format for meeting together, and living arrangements. Thus, he concludes that Christianity represents a combination of 'philosophical school' and 'association' (Wilken 1971:280, 287).[17]

In "Patrons and Officers in Club and Church" (1977), *L. William Countryman* briefly states that among the analogues available to the ancient public for understanding the early Christian groups were the Jewish synagogue, the Mithraic group and the philosophical schools, but the best analogue, particularly in the early empire, was the voluntary association. Recognizing that this is not a new thought, Countryman attempts to push the analogy further by using it as "a tool to explore the church's inner life" (1977:135). After briefly describing the associations, he notes that the Christian churches were not "typical" Greco-Roman associations, and that some differences exist. However, aspects of the church such as its restricted but voluntary membership, its worship of a heroized man, its common meals and its reliance on rich members to support the poor[18] would all suggest to the outsider that Christian groups were, in essence, associations (1977:136–37).

The differences between association and church lie in a number of areas. Although the rich were required to assist the poor, they were not honored for doing so in the way they were lauded in the associations. There exists few Christian inscriptions honoring patrons, in contrast to the many inscriptions honoring association patrons and benefactors. He also states (1977:138) that each association, due to its being a "strictly local institution," was "firmly enmeshed in the social order of its city," with no outside authority higher than the patron.[19] The Christian groups, on the other hand, had greater extralocal links and had a higher authority (i.e., links to Jesus as founder or "god") outside of the local congregation, either literally or in theory.[20] Thus, like the associations, the church's financial support came from its rich members but, unlike the associations, those with authority were its ministers, not always the same persons as the patrons.[21] As a result of his study, Countryman concludes that "the early church was both a club and something other than a club" (1977:140). Its associationlike features allowed it to have a social analogy for those ancients who entered into membership. Its nonassociationlike features allowed it to develop in its own way, eventually forming its own identifying features outside that of the association analogy.

Once again we can turn to **Wayne A. Meeks'** influential *The First Urban Christians* (1983). Meeks points to a number of similarities between voluntary associations and Christian churches. First, both were small groups with intensive face-to-face interactions. Second, membership was established by a free decision to associate, rather than by virtue of birth, although factors of ethnic connection, rank, office and profession sometimes came into play. Third, both attributed importance to rituals and cultic activities, common meals and "fraternal" activities. Fourth, the burial rules and commemorations for the deceased of the voluntary association and references such as 1 Thessalonians 4:13–5:11 or 1 Corinthians 15:29 suggest that both had a concern for the burial of the dead. Fifth, both were dependent upon the beneficence of wealthy patrons. Finally, both seem to have the semblance of democratic internal governance, imitating the classical *polis* in organization, elections and decision making, although in the Christian groups this was complicated by the role of the charismatic spirit.

Meeks also notes a number of differences between voluntary associations and the Christian congregations. First, the Christian groups were exclusive and totalistic in ways not found in professional or religious associations. "Baptized into Christ" meant that the sect was the primary group for the members and demanded primary allegiance (cf. Judaism). Christian groups were not segmented. They were concerned with "salvation" in a comprehensive sense, while voluntary associations were primarily concerned with fellowship and conviviality (feasting, drinking), with some specific cultic functions. Second, Christian groups were more inclusive in terms of social stratification than were the voluntary associations. Meeks suggests that the associations tended to draw together people who were generally socially homogeneous, while the Christian groups allowed for more equality within a group of varying social categories. Third, there was a complete absence of any common terminology between voluntary associations and the Christian groups. Fourth, the voluntary associations did not have the "extralocal linkages" which characterize the Christian movement. Each association was a self-contained local phenomenon.[22] Elsewhere Meeks suggests that the associations were not interested in instructing their members in ethical principles, while the Christian groups concerned themselves with the behavior of their members (1986:114). In the end, these differences prove too great for Meeks; he seems to find the best analogy to the Christian groups in the synagogues (Meeks 1983:80; see chapter 1).

In an article entitled "The Agrippinilla Inscription: Religious Associations and Early Church Formation" in the 1993 *Festschrift* for John Hurd, **Bradley H. McLean** finds a mid-second-century C.E. inscription from a voluntary association in Rome to be particularly instructive as an analogy for early Christianity, particularly in its organizational model, internal structures, membership and recruitment. This large association of over four hundred members was actually grounded in one household, as were various early Christian groups. It had been moved from Mitylene to the Roman Campagna *en masse* and, there, seems to have attracted some new adherents from those who came into contact with the head of the household and his wife (Gallicanus and Agrippinilla). In a similar fashion, Christianity proved itself to be quite portable throughout the empire. Like the early church, this association was of mixed membership, male and female, slaves, freedmen and masters. Its use of titles was extensive, but differed greatly from those used in other associations dedicated to Dionysus, reflecting an experimentation with titles found also in the churches.

In the same volume, ***John S. Kloppenborg*** contributed an article entitled "Edwin Hatch, Churches and Collegia" (1993a) on the topic of voluntary associations, in which he sketches the early development of the use of the associations as an analogy for Christian groups. His particular interest is Edwin Hatch, whose work he thinks to be "sometimes maligned but mostly neglected" (1993a:212). Kloppenborg traces the history of the critique of Hatch and suggests that it was based more on the theological considerations of the scholars than on an evaluation of the data presented by Hatch. In particular, Kloppenborg suggests that many scholars could not tolerate the suggestion that the church owed its structure to paganism. Although a number of scholars conceded the point that the churches might have looked like the associations to outsiders, few would agree that they had been influenced by them. Instead, they looked to Judaism for influences on Paul's thinking and on Pauline church structure. Kloppenborg makes it clear that, to his mind, this has apologetic overtones and is not based on the evidence from antiquity— "Not only did Christian organizations *appear* to be *collegia;* there is a strong likelihood that they thought of themselves as such" (1993a:228, his emphasis).

Kloppenborg also points out that, despite what his opponents thought him to be saying, Hatch was not suggesting the influence of the associations on the Christian groups (that is, that there was a genealogical connection), but merely that there is an analogical connection, wherein to understand one group helps to understand the other. Specifically, Kloppenborg suggests that the analogy can help scholars understand the ways in which the churches were situated within Roman society; the ways in which they offered benefits, both religious and social, to members; and the way members of the groups related to one another and to "outsiders," both on an individual as well as an institutional level.

Kloppenborg also discusses some of the modern scholars who have seriously considered the voluntary associations (1993a:220–24). He is particularly critical of Wayne Meeks (1983), whom Kloppenborg thinks has misread the evidence when Meeks notes four differences between the associations and Christian groups (see above). Kloppenborg (1993a:231–37) effectively takes Meeks to task on the first three of these differences. In terms of technical designations used to refer to the associations, Kloppenborg suggests that the term *ekklēsia* would have been understood in the urban context of Paul's churches to indicate a voluntary association. Names for officers within the churches were as diverse as those within the associations, and one should not expect to find uniformity in either. Membership within both types of "groups" was inclusive to some degree, although Kloppenborg suggests that the "inclusivity" of Paul's churches has been as exaggerated as the exclusivity of associations.

Meeks' fourth "difference," that of the local nature of the associations and the "worldwide" nature of Christianity, is not addressed directly by Kloppenborg (but see Kloppenborg 1996a:27–28, n. 19). However, I have addressed this issue (Ascough 1997) in an article that suggests that both the voluntary associations and the early Christian assemblies were primarily locally-based groups with limited translocal links, and that the "difference" in this area has been overstated.

In the end, Kloppenborg strongly advocates the use of the voluntary associations as an analogy for understanding "the internal dynamics and the remarkable successes of the Pauline churches," with the hope that, in so doing, it will lead to "new and productive approaches for understanding the organization of early Christian churches" (1993a:238). An essay published by Kloppenborg in the same year (1993b) attempts to do just that by reading 1 Thessalonians 4:9–12 in light of a church organized along the lines of a voluntary association, comprised mainly of poor, Gentile handworkers (esp. 1993b:274–77).

A more recently published essay by Kloppenborg explores the analogy further. In "Egalitarianism in the Myth and Rhetoric of Pauline Churches" (1996b) Kloppenborg begins on the assumption that "it is *a priori* likely that Christians in the cities of the eastern empire would have instinctively organized themselves on the pattern" of the Hellenistic voluntary associations, and thus "the social dynamics in play in these groups is likely to have also characterized Pauline groups" (1996b:253; cf. 1996a:23). Turning to 1 Corinthians 6:1–11, Kloppenborg shows how Paul's injuction against taking one another to court betrays a problem within the Corinthian congregation which is common within the voluntary associations.

Legal action of the sort described in 1 Corinthians 6 presupposes that both parties were from the wealthy strata of society. Civil cases were brought to the courts by such people as a means of displaying status; "[t]he courts, as instruments of social control, were one way in which superior social status was displayed and maintained" in a public forum (1996b:255–56). Paul's charge in 1 Corinthians 6 aims to curb such displays of competition for honor among the wealthy of the congregation. The regulations of a number of voluntary associations show that regularly occurring agonistic community interaction required that restrictions be placed on members who were challenging one another's honor, both during the meetings of the association and outside of the meetings, by taking one another to court. Thus we see a marked similarity between the Corinthian Christians and the voluntary associations in terms of both internal conflict among members and regulated conflict resolution.[23]

For Kloppenborg, the primary difference between the Christian groups and the associations lies in another area of competion for honor, that of benefaction. Displays of benefaction were strongly encouraged in the regulations of the associations with the promise of greater honors for the most generous. Such competition does not seem to have been promoted in the Pauline Christian groups. Instead, fictive kinship was created within the groups through the use of familial metaphors (e.g., *adelphos,* "brothers and sisters") which at least attempted to introduce a sense of equality into the group.[24]

Two other studies warrant brief mention. ***Caroline F. Whelan*** (1993) has shown that women were not only active members of voluntary associations but often served as patrons of associations. This information is used to show how Paul's reference to Phoebe in Romans 16:1–2 as both *diakonos* and *prostatis* has often been misunderstood to indicate that she is "merely" a "deaconess" and "helper," and thus inferior in status to male leaders in the group. Rather, these words have the unambigious meaning of "deacon" and "patron" respectively. Moreover, since women commonly functioned as such in the voluntary associations, it is likely that Phoebe fulfills such roles in the Christian communities, not only for Paul and the church at Cenchreae, but for many others also.

My own narrowly focused study (***Ascough*** 1996) examines the use of the verb *epiteleō* ("complete"; "fulfill") in 2 Corinthians 8:1–15 and in the inscriptions of the voluntary associations. In the latter, the word is used for the performance of sacred rites, for the fulfillment of oaths made to the gods and to indicate benefactions of various kinds. When Paul uses *epiteleō* in urging the Corinthians to contribute money to his collection for the Jerusalem church he is thus appealing to the Corithians' sense of religious duty.

In the first monograph treatment of voluntary associations and Pauline Christianity to appear in recent times, *Hierarchie und Egalität: Eine sozialgeschichtliche Untersuchung paulinischer Gemeinden und griechisch-römischer Vereine* (1995 [*Hierarchy and Equality: A Social-historical Investigation of Pauline Communities and Greco-Roman Associations*]), **Thomas Schmeller** examines social relationships and patronage at Corinth in light of social practices within voluntary associations. His object is to determine whether the patterns reflected in the Corinthian community are antithetical to or compatible with social relationships found in the voluntary association. (1995:9–10).[25]

Schmeller begins with a brief survey of research into the comparison of Christianity and the associations. He divides his discussion into two parts, dealing first with scholarship around the turn of the twentieth century (primarily Heinrici and Hatch [see above] and two of their detractors, C. Holsten and J. Weiß), and then with scholarship since 1970 (utilizing the brief comments of Meeks 1983:77–80).

The second part of the book begins with an introductory section on rank and status and patronage and clientage in the Greco-Roman world (1995:19–24). This leads him to a fuller discussion of associations, with a clear emphasis on the social location of typical members (lower rank and status) and their dependence on nonmember patrons for such things as social protection, money for food and wine for banquets, and buildings in which to meet.

In outlining his source of information for voluntary associations, Schmeller focuses primarily on four texts: *SIG*[3] 985, 1109, *ILS* II/2 7212, 7213.[26] Having shown how these inscriptions are generally representative of voluntary associations in the Roman empire in terms of attraction, legal status, and purpose and function (1995:27–32), Schmeller goes on to describe the basic structure of associations in terms of patrons, officials and membership (1995:33–53). He concludes that associations could have both a hierarchical and egalitarian character—hierarchical with respect to a privileged position for patrons and officers, and egalitarian with respect to the general membership of the association. Such a mixture not only reflects the social structure of the dominant cultural milieu (hierarchical), but also provides some escape from it (egalitarianism).

With a careful awareness of the difference between Paul's view of his community expressed in 1 Corinthians and the actual social situation (1995:54; cf. Kloppenborg 1996b:260), Schmeller turns in the third part of his book to an analysis of the Corinthian church. There he finds a similar set of social relationships at work when he examines patronage relationships, church offices and the status of the individual members. Like the voluntary associations, the Corinthian church received the patronage of wealthier persons, and such patrons were granted a larger portion of food at community meals. Differences with the associations lie in the area of terminology for patrons,[27] the inclusion of patrons in the association itself,[28] and in the rewards given for patronage (1995:73–74).[29]

In the Corinthian community, unlike the associations, there was no clearly defined layer of officials between the patrons and the general membership, and certainly no uniformity of functions and titles. Instead, one finds a number of general descriptions of functionaries among the membership, with no clearly fixed boundaries (1 Cor 11–14, esp. 12:27–31; 1995:78). In terms of the status of members, Schmeller suggests that the Christian ideal of social equality[30] was being threatened by two conflicts at Corinth: lawsuits among members of higher status (1 Cor 6) and the "strong/weak" debate between the minority higher status and the majority lower status members (1 Cor 8–10). This ideal of general equality within the "body of Christ" goes far beyond the egalitarianism experienced in the voluntary associations (1995:92–93).

Schmeller's study shows that reading 1 Corinthians against the background of the voluntary associations sheds light on the social relationships within the Corinthian community. In particular, it shows that both groups had characteristics of hierarchy and egalitarianism, where the wealthy acted as patrons and consequently received greater privileges. However, in the end the Corinthian community is shown to be different from the associations in terms of its treatment of its patrons, its lack of officials, and its ideal (if not practice) of total equality among members.

Schmeller's book is a helpful introduction, both for its summary of the characteristics of Greco-Roman voluntary associations and its utilization of these in a study of a particular Pauline Christian group.[31] It is unfortunate that it is marred by a few omissions. The first is Schmeller's choice to focus primarily on four inscriptions, as these are the most frequently cited inscriptions in discussions of voluntary associations and early Christianity. While it is true that these inscriptions have much to teach us, a much greater database of inscriptions is available, literally in the thousands (Kloppenborg 1996a:23). Unfortunately, many remain untranslated and, as in this case, often unconsulted. A wider database would have helped nuance Schmeller's arguments.[32] Second, while Schmeller does have some secondary material from as late as 1995, he has missed three important articles all published in one volume: Cotter 1993, McLean 1993 and Kloppenborg 1993a. These articles would have helped inform Schmeller's arguments on a number of points, especially in his uncritical acceptance of Meeks' four "differences" between voluntary associations and Christian groups, three of which Kloppenborg addresses effectively (see above).[33] Nevertheless, it is hoped that Schmeller's book will prove to be the beginning of a much wider, and much more thorough, exploration of the voluntary associations and early Christian groups.

At a number of points Schmeller builds on the work of ***Hans-Josef Klauck,*** another important German scholar who uses the voluntary associations as a comparative group for understanding early Christianity. Klauck has most often described the associations as the background for understanding Christian house churches (see 1981a:11; 1981b:86–87; 1992:32–34) and the Lord's Supper (see 1982, esp. 68–71).

Conclusion

This brings us to the end of our survey of voluntary associations as a model for early Christianity and also our survey of the models of community formation more generally. As with the other models, the survey of scholarship has shown that the model of voluntary associations can be used profitably as an analogy for understanding early Pauline church formation. However, as some of the writers have pointed out, it is by no means a perfect analogy. Some of the particular objections have been addressed by other scholars, although not everyone will find the latter arguments compelling.

Nevertheless, more so than for the other models, it is perhaps too early to pass final judgment on the model of voluntary associations. Much of the material remains in obscure, inaccessible works and many of the primary sources, the inscriptions, remain untranslated. Most references to the associations rely on earlier, often outdated works and, as Robert Wilken observes, they are often "endless, very repetitive, and frequently preoccupied with questions of legal history" (1971:290 n. 35). Too often the same few inscriptions are presented as evidence in the arguments.

A current research project at the Toronto School of Theology hopes to rectify this situation in the near future with a two-volume work provisionally entitled *Cultic Groups, Guilds, and Collegia: Associations in the Greco-Roman World,* edited by John S. Kloppenborg and Bradley H. McLean. The second volume will prove particularly useful, as it will include a number of texts and English translations, along with bibliography, from associations throughout the Greco-Roman world. Easier access to the primary data should allow for a more fruitful debate over the use of voluntary associations as a model for understanding early Christianity.

Conclusion

We have now reached the conclusion of our survey of models of Pauline community formation. Having examined the four models of synagogues, philosophical schools, ancient mysteries and voluntary associations, it should be clear that no one model is adequate in and of itself for explaining all aspects of Paul's Christian communities. To begin with, the strong, universal missionizing tendency seems to have been unique to Christianity, although all the groups did have procedures whereby they grew numerically by attracting new adherents. Once the community was formed, the models become more helpful in explaining some aspects of some communities. However, there is no way of fitting every one of the churches to which Paul writes under the rubric of any one of the models proposed. To attempt to do so more likely reflects a modern desire to systematize the past than the realities of the situation in the mid-first century C.E.

However, it is hoped that our survey will encourage the broadest possible comparison between the Pauline Christian groups and other groups in the first century. Clearly, early Christian groups can be shown to have similarities to a number of different social groups in antiquity and yet still have some distinct characteristics. Thus, the Christian groups were not exactly the same as any of the other groups in antiquity, yet at the same time the Christian groups were not entirely different. On the general level, understanding a broad range of these groups will help us to better understand the nature of Paul's churches and how they were formed.

While most modern scholars acknowledge in theory the lack of a uniform local model for the church, in practice this importance has been overlooked. In general, scholarship which undertakes a social description of "Pauline Christianity" homogenizes all Pauline churches, generally treating 1 Corinthians as the model for all else. This is both historically implausible and methodologically problematic. Failure to take seriously local peculiarities of each of Paul's churches and to read each of his letters in the light of the local social situation to which each was addressed will result in a misunderstanding of that particular Christian community.

At this point it would serve us well to examine briefly the methodological study of *Jonathan Z. Smith, Drudgery Divine: On the Comparison of Early Christianities and the Religions of Late Antiquity* (1990). It may seem odd to discuss methodology at the end of a book rather than the beginning, however this is necessitated by the fact that Smith's book has only recently been published and thus his thinking was not available to many of the authors we have discussed. A second justification for discussing Smith's work here is the significance of his work for proposing a possible way forward for studying Paul's communities in light of first-century associative models.

Smith's erudite book will repay reading and rereading in its entirety. Here we will simply highlight some of his most salient points. Smith begins by tracing the origins of the modern comparative religions approach, suggesting that too often polemical agendas have been the context of the discussion and have skewed both the presentation of the "facts" and the subsequent analyses and conclusions.[1]

Smith goes on to suggest that a more rigorously helpful approach will not emphasize the "uniqueness" of Jesus and early Christianity. Rather, the focus will be on "difference, a complex term which invites negotiation, classification and comparison" (1990:42). Comparison is not a matter of identifying one thing as another; i.e., "Christianity is a mystery religion."[2] Such statements too often have been the focus of scholarship, which assumes that comparison of Christianity to another group is a matter of showing both "direct relations (borrowing and dependency)" and "prestigious origins (pedigree)" (1990:47). That is, its primary concern is genealogical.

In place of this approach, Smith advocates analogical comparison. Data compared analogically does not aim to find direct connections. Instead, analogy serves to highlight similarities and differences among a limited set of options. The analogy rests in the mind of the scholar conducting the investigation and helps one to understand how things might be conceived or redescribed. It is "a disciplined exaggeration in the service of knowledge" (1990:52). Through such a comparative method of emphasizing similarities and differences, the scholar gains a perspective on the material which leads to a more nuanced analysis of the material than simply postulating genealogical relationships.[3]

Smith (1990:51) proposes the following formula for discussing comparisons:

x resembles *y* more than *z* with respect to…

Relationships are thus seen as being three-way relationships, which does not rule out the possibility of secondary analogy of "*z*," but places the emphasis on what is most analogous in a specific category of comparison. Placing this in the context of our investigation, I would suggest that a much more profitable way forward in the future would be statements such as:

The Philippian Christian community (*x*) resembles the Macedonian voluntary associations (*y*) more than the synagogues (*z*) with respect to its internal organization.[4]

Such statements will obviously demand much of those who make them, requiring study of particular associative groups in particular locations and using this information to enlighten our understanding of a particular letter of Paul. No longer will it be possible to make broad, sweeping statements about "Pauline community formation" in general. However, this will lead to a much more nuanced understanding of Paul's Christian communities and of each of his letters, and will repay the effort required to undertake such detailed investigations.

From our own survey of the scholarly literature in the area of Pauline community formation and the methodological discussion of Smith, we might conclude that a different associative model might be appropriate for a different locale. For example, as already mentioned, the Christian communities at Philippi and Thessalonica might be more easily categorized as voluntary associations since there is no evidence of synagogues in the area, the language does not reflect clearly a philosophical school or the mysteries, and there is little indication of the familial structure of the house churches. However, the Corinthian congregation, with its many divisions (1 Cor 1:11–12), might better be understood as a collection of house churches (Filson 1939:111), some of whom understood themselves to be philosophical schools. The churches in Galatia, with their emphasis on the law, might have been more inclined to use the synagogue for their organizational model, at least until Paul writes to them to redirect their attention away from the law. However, these musings require much more detailed investigation, and hold the way forward for the future study of Pauline community formation.

By way of conclusion, we might briefly address the implications of the study of Pauline community formation for the contemporary church. It should be clear that Paul's communities were neither based on one specific analogical model, nor was each Pauline community the same.[5] Each community was truly locally based and thus part of its context. Although united under the founder-figure of Paul, they were autonomous groups and reflect a number of differences from one another.

Nevertheless, it is the aim of responsible New Testament scholarship not simply to show as false the notion of early Christianity as a glorious time of pristine theology and social harmony—the "good old days," which are looked back upon as the model that the modern churches must replicate in order to be truly Christian. Instead, New Testament scholarship must set the early Christian communities in a more responsible context, one which emphasizes both that they reflected the environment within which they were first formed, and the fact that they also adapted to the various situations which Christians faced in the early period.

Christians did not invent the idea of groups, nor did the concept of a "Christian" group suddenly appear from above. Rather, Christians were able to look to the various groups around them as models for group formation, while at the same time adding their own variations to the group structure chosen. In this way they were experimental, nonstandardized, and genuinely "incarnational." As God took on human form in the person of Jesus of Nazareth, so also the church took on the forms of ancient groups already in place. As a result, the contemporary experimentation in the formation of Christian communities in various locales worldwide is not a transgression of a "biblical" model of what it is to be a "church." Rather, inherent to the earliest period of Christian formation (as shown in our canonical texts) is a view that Christian communities experiment and modify in order to represent a commitment to the tradition handed down by the "founders" alongside a willingness to adapt to the social situation of local believers.

Notes

Introduction

1. For the most part, we will discuss "the mysteries" rather than "mystery religions." The latter term evokes a sense of exclusive adherence to one group which simply was not the case. Whereas Judaism, Christianity and Islam are religions insofar as they reflect a strong communal association and one cannot claim allegiance to more than one at any given time, in antiquity one could be initiated into a number of mysteries and be a member of one or more of the affiliated groups. For further discussion see Burkert 1987:1–4, 53. The term "mystery religions" was commonly used (with the attendant assumptions) by scholars in the earlier part of this century.

2. It is important to keep in mind that many of these scholars would readily admit that although their model predominates in their understanding of Paul, other models may also have been influential in the formation of Paul's communities.

3. Paul himself does not help matters by not referring to the church using any of the terms regularly used of the groups with which we are concerned (*synagōguē, philosophia, thiasos, synados, koinon, mysteria*). Instead, he uses the word *ekklēsia,* a word which has more to do with politics than private associations (Branick 1989:27). Yet this term itself is used as a descriptor within all of the other groupings.

4. We might also make note here of a related topic which will occupy some of our attention in this book—Paul's relationship to his communities as founder and/or teacher. This will be discussed insofar as it suggests a definite model of community formation. There are some

works available that discuss Paul's relationship to his communities, but without specifying a community model. For example, J. Paul Sampley (1980) suggests that Paul created a legally recognized partnership (a *societas Christi*) with some (but not all) of his converts (namely, the Philippians and Philemon). However, Sampley's explanation does not detail actual community structure so much as Paul's possible relationship with the communities. Sampley's work was not well received (see the summary of his detractors' arguments in Witherington 1994:118–19; cf. the reviews of D. M. Sweetland, *CBQ* 44 [1982] 689–90 and A. C. Wire, *JBL* 101 [1982] 468–69), but has found recent supporters in Capper 1993 and Bormann 1995.

5. For a more detailed survey of the evidence for house churches in the New Testament see Branick 1989:13–35, 58–77.

6. In Corinth, as elsewhere, the "entire church" of the city was composed of a number of smaller congregations from around the city; see Branick 1989:23–28.

7. On the size and patterns of various types of families in antiquity see Hanson 1989:142–51.

8. Clearly not everyone in the household would necessarily be content with the new allegiance, thus creating social tensions (see Meeks 1983:76–77). Such was probably the case with Onesimus in Philemon's household, who, despite his master's conversion to Christianity, was not a Christian when he met Paul at a later date.

9. See White 1990:111–23. Blue (1994:138–71) gives summary details of archaeological sites in Palestine, Syria, Corinth and Rome. For more details on Roman sites, also see Petersen 1969:265–71 and Jeffers 1991, esp. 63–89.

10. This anticipated the basilical architecture of Constantine (White 1990:4–5). However, White (1990:24) is careful to point out that overall there was a "subtle process of architectural adaptation through incremental renovation of existing structures" rather than radical and deliberate changes.

11. Branick self-admittedly owes much to the works of Robert Banks (1981, now 1994) and Hans-Josef Klauck (1981b; cf. 1981a, 1982). Both of these authors are worthy of consideration by anyone pursuing the investigation of the house churches in the New Testament.

12. He also admits some (limited) parallels between the voluntary associations and the local Christian communities; 1989:46–49.

13. See further, Klauck 1981a:11; 1981b:86–87; 1992:32–34; Kloppenborg 1996a:23; cf. White 1990:32–47, 141; McLean 1993: 247–49.

14. See Klauck 1981a:13–14; 1981b:95–97; cf. Kee 1990:8–14; White 1990:62–77.

15. White 1990:47–58.

16. Stowers 1984:66–68; De Witt 1954a:93, 52. Stowers (1984) argues that the primary location of Paul's missionary preaching and subsequent teaching was private homes rather than public places. In this, Paul was like many of the philosophers of his day.

1. Synagogues

1. See the detailed investigation by Kee 1995a.

2. Goodman (1994:109–53) argues that the rise of a more active Jewish mission in the second century and beyond was a direct result of the influence of the universal proselytizing mission of early Christianity. He suggests that the missionary impulse arose within and out of Christianity itself. Its exact origins are difficult to trace, but probably stem from an eschatological fervor, the particular personality of the apostle Paul, the disappointment over the delay of the Parousia (1994:167–68), and the inter-Christian debate over the admission of the Gentiles into the church (1994:170).

3. See also MacLennan and Kraabel 1986; cf. Wilcox 1981. A number of Kraabel's essays, including this one, are republished in Overman and MacLennan 1992.

4. There is some archaeological evidence, but it tends to be later than the first century (e.g., Nock 1972a:51, n. 2), as well as discussions of sympathizers, proselytes and converts in rabbinic literature (cf. Feldman 1986:62).

5. On the Sardis synagogue, Kraabel remains unconvinced that there were large numbers of "semi-converts" or "God-fearers" (1994:79, contra Feldman). To be sure, Gentiles interacted with Jews in the Roman Empire, but often for reasons of business, politics, or friendship, rather than "religion" (Kraabel 1994:81, 82; cf. 79). The Diaspora Jews would have expressed themselves in the language, concepts,

images, ideas, forms, etc. with which they were most familiar, that of the dominant Hellenistic culture (Kraabel 1994:84). When faced with such evidence there is no need to posit "proselytes."

6. The description as such is most likely a Lukan addition to Q; see Kloppenborg 1988:50.

7. See Feldman (1986), who responds to Kraabel (and Mac-Lennan), although most of his examples are later than the first century C.E.; Segal 1990:93–96, esp. 95. Segal admits that Luke's agenda may have effected his depiction, but suggests that "God-fearers nonetheless existed, possibly in large numbers" (1990:95).

8. For an analysis of Gager, see Smith 1978.

9. Gager explicitly rejects the mysteries (1975:129) and the philosophical schools (1975:134–35) as valid models for understanding early Christian formation. In fact, he claims that had Christianity adopted the institutional pattern of one of these other groups, it would not have survived much past the first century (1975:129; 134).

10. He does allow that the synagogues were "construed legally as collegia and adopted many aspects of collegial structure" (Meeks 1983:80; cf. 35).

11. But see Brooten 1982.

12. Rajak and Noy (1993:77) suggest that Meeks too quickly discounts the synagogues as a model due to the lack of explicit evidence in Paul's letters for Christian imitation of the synagogue. They suggest, Jews and Christians shared many habits (scripture reading, hymn singing, prayers, common meals) and "many problems of principle and practice arising from participation in city life and interaction with idolatrous 'pagans.'" This is explored in more detail in Rajak 1985.

13. He also has a somewhat uncritical understanding of the picture of the expansion of Christianity described in Acts.

14. Lieu (1994:334 and n. 12) acknowledges that this is only true for males and has to admit that it is unclear what the practical and outward distinction between female "God-fearers" and "proselytes" would be.

15. Paul's communities are also "inclusive," but this is a less dominant trait in Paul's letters; it comes through more so in Acts.

16. The Sayings Source is material common to Matthew and Luke but not found in Mark.

17. See also Kee (1990:1–24), who makes the connection between

Christian groups (*ekklēsia*) reflected in the gospels and the emerging rabbinic groups, which adopt the name *synagōguē*.

18. I would certainly not want to discourage this very important dialogue.

2. Philosophical Schools

1. See Trebilco 1994:311–12, n. 87 for details. Malherbe (1983:89–91) understands it to refer to a guild hall, indicating that Paul spoke before a voluntary association.

2. We will focus on Malherbe 1983 and 1987, the earlier work being the groundwork for the latter study. In Malherbe 1989b he has collected some of the studies which underlie his 1987 work (see 1989b:ix).

3. Sociological study of antiquity can focus on social facts or on sociological theory (Malherbe 1983:20). Malherbe's principal focus is social facts or social history.

4. Malherbe (1983:26) points out that, in fact, pagan critics did equate Christianity with Epicureanism in the second century and beyond.

5. See Stowers 1988; Aune 1991; Guerra 1995; Glad 1995, all discussed below. Also see the essays found in Engberg-Pedersen 1995 and Fitzgerald 1996.

6. Much has been written on parallels between Hellenistic philosophy generally and the writings of the New Testament. It is beyond our narrow focus to survey all of this material. A good place to start might be Malherbe 1989 or 1992:271–78. A very helpful resource is the volumes of *Studia ad Corpus Hellenisticum Novi Testamenti,* which are being published by Brill.

7. Cf. Meeks 1983:83. Meeks quotes Marrou (1955:34), who indicates that philosophical schools could be organized along the lines of a voluntary association (*thiasos*) dedicated to the goddess of culture. For more on associations see chapter 4.

8. The ancient philosophers were primarily concerned with the lives of men, although there were some exceptions—e.g., Hypparchia the Cynic; the Epicurean Garden.

9. Nock also suggests that synagogue worship, with its sermons, "would remind outsiders of a philosophical school rather than a temple" (Nock 1933:62). These conclusions do not necessarily turn Paul into a particular type of moral philosopher. As Nock states elsewhere, Paul is not a Stoic; at best he reveals a knowledge of Stoic ideas, but he either opposes them or uses them against Stoicism itself (Nock 1972a:126).

10. He was also skeptical about the existence of a "universal proselytizing mission" within the synagogues of the first century; see chapter 1.

11. Hock (1978:557; cf. 1980:66) rightly rejects the problematic claim that Paul's trade was the result of the rabbinic practice of combining the study of Torah with learning a trade. Such a practice is difficult to establish before the middle of the second century C.E.

12. We will return to this discussion below; suffice it for now to say that, at least in Thessalonica, there are indications that the church was formed like a trade association (see 1 Thess 4:9–12; cf. Kloppenborg 1993b:274–77).

13. For more on Stoic influences on Paul, see Bultmann 1956: 185–86.

14. Aune (1991:283) points out that while the philosophical school was the appropriate place for the diatribe in the case of some philosophers (Epictetus, Musonius Rufus), it was not the case with others who were aiming at much broader audiences for mass-conversion purposes (Maximus of Tyre, Plutarch, Dio Chrysostom).

15. Aune has argued elsewhere in favor of a greater awareness on behalf of scholars of Paul's use of philosophical concepts and language. See, for example, Aune 1995.

16. See also Simpson (1941), who suggests that Epicureans and Christians were often associated with one another in popular understanding. Members of both groups were considered to be atheists (Simpson 1941:372) and, we might add, "heretics" (cf. the Jewish Birkat ha-Minim).

17. De Witt maintains that the translation "elemental spirits" is a mistranslation; the word *stoicheia* is better translated simply "elements" or "basic principles."

18. Epicurean communities were based on the household and strove to reproduce among members the relationships of the household (De Witt 1954a:93, 52).

19. In an earlier essay De Witt (1936) describes the organization of Epicurean groups, which had perhaps broad similarities to Christian groups, but varied greatly in detail. The differences in detail are somewhat minimized in an essay from 1944.

20. For more on psychagogy, see Malherbe 1987:81–88; 1990: 375–91; 1992:301–4.

21. Other recent investigations of Paul's use of Stoic notions include Martens 1994. For a historical survey of those who have made the connection between Stoicism and the New Testament, see Colish 1992.

22. Engberg-Pedersen goes on to show that when Paul uses the language of hierarchy in order to give structure to the Philippian congregation, along with his use of emotional force in his rhetoric, he is no longer arguing like a Stoic (1995:280–89). However, "it is when Paul is at his most Stoic that he is also at his most Christian" (1995:280, cf. 289).

23. The first point is tenuous at best—we may not possess literature from the assocations, but that might be an accident of time. Most associations claimed a patron deity, many of whom did have much literary support which may have been used by the associations. The second point is simply wrong—some associations did have translocal links much like those of Christianity (see Ascough 1997).

3. The Ancient Mysteries

1. For a discussion of the use of "mysteries" rather than "mystery religions," see footnote 1 in the Introduction.

2. Other passages often highlighted are 1 Cor 2:14; 1 Cor 15:1–58; Phil 2:6–11, although none so much as Rom 6:1–11.

3. Unfortunately, what is known is often too little to draw certain conclusions. The experiences and interpretations of the rites were generally well-kept secrets by the initiates. What is known is generally taken from inscriptions and works of art aimed at the general public and thus is rather vague on details (Wedderburn 1982:829).

4. For a comprehensive, classified bibliography of the mysteries up to 1979 see Metzger 1984.

5. Voluntary associations are not limited to this type, and a much broader understanding will be discussed in chapter 4.

6. We are most interested in the influence of the mysteries on Pauline community formation. An investigation of a more general influence on Paul's thinking is beyond the scope of this chapter. Those who want to pursue this would do well to begin with the works of Metzger 1968 or Wagner 1967 and follow the bibliographical suggestions made therein.

7. Metzger 1968:8; Lease 1980:1315–16. Among the church fathers are Justin Martyr, Tertullian, Origen, Firmicus Maternus, and Jerome. The non-Christians include Celsus and Flavius Vopiscus.

8. This was the case with the eucharist and the similar rite in Mithraism. Justin Martyr (*Apologia* 1.64.4; *Dialogus cum Tryphone Judaeo* 70.1) and Tertullian (*De Praescriptione Haereticorum* 40) attribute the similarities to demons.

9. See Riches 1993:31–49 for a survey of the influence of the history-of-religions school on Pauline scholarship.

10. The German original, *Die hellenistischen Mysterien-religionen,* first appeared in 1910. The English translation of 1978 is based on the third edition, published in German in 1926.

11. Reitzenstein looks to the Isis mystery of Apuleius to explain Paul's view of baptism in Romans 6.

12. Many scholars now consider Reitzenstein's approach to be simplistic and reductionistic. He "depicted mysticism as a unified phenomenon that culminated in Gnosticism in the second and subsequent centuries C.E." (Kee 1995b:145).

13. Loisy recognizes that the transformation was not effected by Paul alone, but he "was the most important worker in this metamorphosis" (1911:57).

14. This book underwent five editions, the last in 1964, under the guidance of colleagues of Bousset, who died before the publication of the second volume. However, it was not translated into English until 1970.

15. English translation of *Das Urchristentum in Rahmen der Antiken Religionen* (Zurich: Artemis, 1949).

16. Bultmann maintains that the work of Jesus himself was conceived along the lines of a Gnostic redeemer myth. He goes on to suggest that Paul can describe Jesus' death and resurrection variously, using

concepts from Judaism (Rom 3:25), from the mysteries (Rom 6:2–11), and from Gnosticism (2 Cor 5:17; see 1956:197).

17. Developments in our understanding of the mysteries have come through archaeological finds, including discoveries of actual meeting places, and retrievals of new literary texts. Other texts have been reassessed and reinterpreted. Despite this, however, what took place in the actual rites of the mysteries remains enigmatic (Wiens 1980:1255).

18. Many of Nock's essays have been collected and published together in a two-volume work. Since this is the most accessible for most students, we have referred to the pagination of the essays in this larger work.

19. See also Kennedy 1913, esp. 115–98. Kennedy sees the most obvious background to Paul's language in the Old Testament (1913:154–55). Hugo Rahner (1963) agrees that Paul's language was not influenced by the mysteries, although he does admit that there is some general terminological affinity with the mysteries.

20. However, Nock probably overstates his case when he claims that Paul is only aware of paganism in a very general way, and that there was no possible way that Paul would appropriate concepts from it (Malherbe 1989a:13 responding to 1972d:930).

21. Nock's position has more recently been challenged by Jonathan Z. Smith, who points out a number of methodological flaws and apologetic predispositions in Nock's work (Smith 1990:66–84).

22. English translation of *Das religionsgeschichtliche Problem von Römer 6, 1–11* (Abhandlungen zur Theologie des Alten und Neuen Testaments 39; Zürich: Zwingli, 1962).

23. The first part of Wagner's book presents one of the most comprehensive surveys of the understanding of Romans 6 by the practitioners of the history-of-religions school.

24. Wedderburn 1982:817 citing C. Colpe in *Gnomon* 38 (1966) 48.

25. Wedderburn is critical of some aspects of Wagner's study, particularly the fact that Wagner "makes no allowance for Paul's use, or modification, of Christian tradition" when discussing Romans 6 (Wedderburn 1982:818).

26. A much more thorough and recent work, and to my mind a

much more helpful work, is Jonathan Z. Smith's *Drudgery Divine* (1990). However, Smith's methodolgical reflections have important implications for our entire project, so his work will be summarized in the Conclusion.

27. Metzger has not gone unchallenged, most recently (and most effectively) by Smith 1990:48–50.

28. For an extensive methodological treatment of the comparison of Christianity and the mysteries see Smith 1990. Smith's work points to the need for a completely new approach to Paul and the mysteries (1990:143). See further on Smith in the Conclusion.

29. In an earlier book Maccoby (1986) argues that Paul was not born a Jew and Pharisee, but was, in fact, an uneasy convert to Judaism.

30. Maccoby goes on to show how this resulted in Paul becoming the foundation for Christian antisemitism (1991:84–89). Christian anti-semitism is the primary concern of his book.

31. Betz makes the connection more broadly to the New Testament texts, but our attention will be those inscriptions which resonate with the texts of the genuine Pauline letters.

32. That is, that it transcends the national boundaries of the Judaism from which it arose; cf. Nock 1972a:70–71.

33. Betz provides ample evidence for making the claim of Paul as founder figure, including many examples from the Hellenistic period. Interestingly, he suggests that Paul's churches were founded as "religious associations" (1995:88–89) or what we have termed voluntary associations. However, he quickly moves on in suggesting that following the founding there was the much longer process of "building the house of the church community" (1995:89). It is in this later aspect that Betz sees the influence of the mysteries.

34. Cf. the earlier work of Edson (1940; 1948) who discusses the cults of Thessalonica without reference to Paul's letters or the early Thessalonian church. In a later article Donfried makes the same case for 2 Thessalonians, although he attributes the writing of that letter to one of Paul's coworkers; Donfried 1993.

35. Holand Hendrix, review, *JBL* 107 (1988) 766; Steven J. Kraftchick, review, *Int* 42 (1988) 412; S.C. Barton, review, *ExpTim* 99/3 (1987) 90.

36. For details see the review by Hendrix 1988:764–65 (cf. Kraftchick's review, 1988:411–12); see previous note.

37. For example, Meeks (1983:74–84) does not include them in his survey of possible models for understanding the formation of the church.

38. In doing so, he is careful to note that, as with Christianity, Mithraism was different over time and in various locales.

4. Voluntary Associations

1. For a more detailed overview see Kloppenborg 1996a or Schmeller 1995:19–53.

2. In the case of Egypt, there is some evidence for associations among the papyri. This confirms what is suggested in the inscriptional record: that associations would have also used other media for their record keeping and correspondence. Unfortunately, such media have not withstood the ravishes of time.

3. On patronage in antiquity generally, see Garnsey and Saller 1987:148–59. For a large collection of translations of inscriptions attesting to the practice of patronage, including some from voluntary associations, see Danker 1982.

4. On women patrons, see Whelan 1993:76–77; Kloppenborg 1996a:25; cf. Meeks 1980:117.

5. The following is a summary of my chapter, "Formation and Propagation of Associations," forthcoming in a two-volume work edited by John S. Kloppenborg and Bradley H. McLean, and provisionally entitled *Cultic Groups, Guilds, and Collegia: Associations in the Ancient World* (in preparation).

6. See Wilken 1971:291, n. 50; cf. Liebenam 1890:272, n. 4.

7. English translation of *Les apôtres* (Histoire des origines du christianisme 2; Paris: Michel Levy, 1866).

8. Hatch's position is summarized in Josaitis 1971:35–40. Renan, Heinrici, and Hatch all underwent strong opposition; see Kloppenborg 1993:217–20; Schmeller 1995:14–16.

9. Cf. Harnack (1887), much influenced by Hatch, who argued similarly that church offices arose from non-Jewish institutions; see Kloppenborg 1993:217.

10. Wilson suggests that they both "had no more than a fraction of our large city congregations of to-day" (1927:125).

11. Wilson rightly notes that all guilds were religious (1927:126).

12. In Christianity, however, it was a closer link via the Holy Spirit.

13. A number of scholars have favorably compared the synagogues to the voluntary associations; Juster 1914:409–13; Smallwood 1981:120–43; Richardson 1996; cf. Meeks 1983:32. Burtchaell (1992:265–67) admits that the associations could easily be seen to be the model for synagogue organization, but he rejects it because of the differences. Ironically, the differences between the Jewish synagogue and the voluntary associations are less striking than those between the Jewish synagogue and the Christian church, yet in this latter he finds a direct genealogical connection. Others have attempted to draw an analogy between the community living at Qumran and voluntary associations; see esp. Weinfeld 1986 and Dombrowski 1966; cf. Marcus 1952. Ramish 1996 also makes the comparison but concludes that they are not analogous.

14. In fact, both these "differences" have been challenged by later writers; Barton and Horsley (1981) show that the social constituency of one group at least was similar to that of the Christian associations. Ascough (1997) argues that both Christian and non-Christian associations were locally based groups with limited translocal links.

15. However, in a work published in the same year (1960a), and in subsequent works, Judge tends to lean towards the philosophical schools as the best analogy for early Christian groups. See chapter 2.

16. He suggests (1971:269) that the self-understanding of the Christians may differ from that of the outsider. He is primarily interested in the view of the outsider. Chapter 2 of *The Christians as the Romans Saw Them* (1984:31–47) contains similar information to the section on "collegia" in the 1971 article.

17. Barton and Horsley (1981:40) support Wilken's view by also concluding that the Christian groups were a combination of a philosophical school and a religious association. More recently Mason (1996) compares philosophical schools with voluntary associations (cf. Klauck 1982:70–71).

18. Countryman spends some time arguing that the church was

not made up primarily of the poor, but included a significant number of rich members, albeit, not of the senatorial class (1977:137).

19. He cites as an exception to this characteristic the guilds of Dionysiac actors (1977:136).

20. Countryman does recognize that the church eventually adapted itself to the pattern of local leadership with its move to the monarchical episcopate (1977:138).

21. This of course led to its own set of problems, which Countryman details. It leads him to conclude that "[t]he formulation of ethical and charitable teachings about wealth was a direct response to tension between club and nonclub patterns within the church" (1977:140).

22. Stambaugh and Balch (1986:141) also recognize that Christian groups could be and would have been compared to voluntary associations in antiquity. Much was shared in common. However, they also highlight the difference of translocal links: "[T]he Christian groups were more conscious of a dynamic connection with a worldwide society of like-minded believers, to a much greater degree than the pagan collegia."

23. In an independent study of 1 Corinthians 6:1–8, Schmeller (1995:86–87) arrives at a similar conclusion, although with less data to support the claim. In fact, Schmeller points more generally to the regulations concerning internal arbitration in Diaspora Jewish groups, the mysteries and voluntary associations (1995:87).

24. Kloppenborg (1996b:260) is careful to point out that Paul's rhetoric aims to reduce conflict and status display but it is unclear to what degree he was successful. That is, we do not know if Pauline groups were "egalitarian."

25. Relationships in Greco-Roman organizations are typically characterized as vertical, hierarchical, and status conscious, while relationships in the Pauline communities are usually said to have been horizontal, egalitarian, and service oriented.

26. These texts are described by Schmeller 1995:26. The texts and a German translation of each are provided in an appendix (1995:96–115). English translations are available for all of them: *SIG*[3] 985 in Barton and Horsley 1981:9–10; *ILS* II/2 7212 (= *CIL* XIV 2112) in MacMullen and Lane 1992:66–69 no. 5.3; *ILS* II/2 7213 (= *CIL* VI

10234) in Gordon 1983:148–49 no. 66; SIG^3 1109 (= IG II^2 1368) in MacMullen and Lane 1992:69–72 no. 5.4.

27. Schmeller argues strongly, although not convincingly, that Paul does not indicate that Phoebe is a "patron" in Rom 16:1–2. See Whelan 1993 (esp. 75–77) for the argument that Phoebe is referred to in the fashion usual for a patron of an association. Oddly, Schmeller does not engage Whelan's work.

28. This is based on his erroneous assumption that patrons did not participate in the patronized association.

29. Schmeller examines Paul's discussion of divisions at Corinth (1 Cor 1–4), the sexual sin of an individual (1 Cor 5), and the Lord's Supper (1 Cor 11) to arrive at these conclusions.

30. This is based on Galatians 3:28, which Schmeller takes as paradigmatic for Paul's ministry.

31. However, although he claims to want to take local peculiarities seriously, Schmeller actually makes Corinth paradigmatic for all Pauline churches (see, for example, 1995:82).

32. To his credit Schmeller (1995:26) recognizes the extent and diversity of the voluntary association inscriptions and explains his use of these particular inscriptions as a means to move quickly to his larger purpose of using the associations as a means to better understand social relationships in the Corinthian community. He does mention some other inscriptions where appropriate. Another unusual oversight on Schmeller's part is his failure to mention the evidence for associations at Corinth. Although such evidence is meager, it is extant (see Ascough 1996:584, n. 3).

33. Even more importantly, Schmeller's conclusions should be read in light of the larger methodological considerations raised by Kloppenborg 1996b.

Conclusion

1. More specifically Smith suggests that the entire endeavor has been tainted by Protestant anti-Catholic apologetics (cf. 1990:34).

2. Smith uses the scholarly literature which discusses the comparison of Christianity and the mysteries to illustrate his method

throughout his book. However, his comments are also apropos for the other models.

3. The use of "analogy" does not rule out some direct influence of any one of these groups on the forming Christian group. However, identifying such influence should not occupy the bulk of any investigation. We should not, in fact, attempt to isolate Christianity from its surroundings but should strive to place it concretely in its Greco-Roman (including Hellenistic Jewish) context (cf. Malherbe 1989a:7). However, one should be aware that too often the "Jewish roots" of Christianity have been used to insulate formative Christianity from its "pagan" surroundings; see Smith 1990:83; Wiens 1980:1251.

4. This statement is meant to be illustrative, not *de facto* the case. However, it is not entirely hypothetical, as it is the burden of my dissertation (Ph.D., University of St. Michael's College, Toronto) to provide the supporting evidence for this claim.

5. It should go without saying that Christian communities founded by others took on characteristics different again from the various Pauline communities, both due to being in a different location and due to the differing perspectives of their own founder figures. For example, Johannine churches cannot be assumed to be of the same structure as those formed by Peter.

Bibliography

Alexander, Loveday. 1995. "Paul and the Hellenistic Schools: The Evidence of Galen." In *Paul in His Hellenistic Context,* ed. Troels Engberg-Pedersen, 60–83. Minneapolis: Fortress.

Anrich, Gustav. 1894. *Das antike Mysterienwesen in seinem Einfluss auf das Christentum.* Göttingen: Vandenhoeck and Ruprecht.

Ascough, Richard S. 1996. "The Completion of a Religious Duty: The Background of 2 Cor 8:1–15." *NTS* 42:584–99.

————. 1997. "Local and Translocal Relationships Among Voluntary Associations and Early Christianity." *JECS* 5:223-41.

Aune, David E. 1991. "Romans as a *Logos Protreptikos.*" In *The Romans Debate: Revised and Expanded Edition,* ed. Karl P. Donfried, 278–96. Peabody: Hendrickson.

————. 1995. "Human Nature and Ethics in Hellenistic Philosophical Traditions and Paul: Some Issues and Problems." In *Paul in His Hellenistic Context,* ed. Troels Engberg-Pedersen, 291–312. Minneapolis: Fortress.

Banks, Robert. 1994. *Paul's Idea of Community: The Early House Churches in Their Cultural Setting.* 2nd edition. Peabody: Hendrickson.

Barton, S. C., and G. H. R. Horsley. 1981. "A Hellenistic Cult Group and the New Testament Churches." *JAC* 24:7–41.

Betz, Hans Dieter. 1968. "The Mithras Inscriptions of Santa Prisca and the New Testament." *NovT* 10:62–80.

————. 1995. "Transferring a Ritual: Paul's Interpretation of Baptism in Romans 6." In *Paul in His Hellenistic Context,* ed. Troels Engberg-Pedersen, 84–118. Minneapolis: Fortress.

Blue, Bradley B. 1994. "Acts and the House Church." In *The Book of Acts in its First Century Setting 2: The Book of Acts in its Graeco-Roman Setting,* 119–222. Grand Rapids and Carlisle: Eerdmans and Paternoster.

Bormann, Lukas. 1995. *Philippi: Staat und Christengemeinde zur Zeit des Paulus.* NovTSup 78. Leiden/New York/Köln.

Borgen, Peder. 1995. "'Yes,' 'No,' 'How Far?': The Participation of Jews and Christians in Pagan Cults." In *Paul in His Hellenistic Context,* ed. Troels Engberg-Pedersen, 30–59. Minneapolis: Fortress.

Bousset, Wilhelm. 1970. *Kyrios Christos.* Nashville: Abingdon.

Branick, Vincent P. 1989. *The House Church in the Writings of Paul.* Zacchaeus Studies: New Testament. Wilmington: Michael Glazier.

Brooten, Bernadette J. 1982. *Women Leaders in Ancient Synagogues: Inscriptional Evidence and Background Issues.* Brown Judaic Studies 36. Chico: Scholars Press.

Bultmann, Rudolf. 1910. *Der Stil der paulinischen Predigt und die kynisch-stoische Diatribe.* Forschungen zur Religion und Literatur des Alten und Neuen Testaments 13. Göttingen: Vandenhoeck & Ruprecht.

———. 1952. *Theology of the New Testament.* Vol. 1. London: SCM.

———. 1956. *Primitive Christianity in Its Contemporary Setting.* London: Thames and Hudson.

Burkert, Walter. 1987. *Ancient Mystery Cults.* Cambridge and London: Harvard University Press.

Burtchaell, James T. 1992. *From Synagogue to Church: Public Services and Offices in the Earliest Christian Communities.* Cambridge and New York: Cambridge University Press.

Capper, Brian J. 1993. "Paul's Dispute with Philippi: Understanding Paul's Argument in Phil 1–2 from His Thanks in 4.10–20." *TZ* 49:193–214.

Casaubon, Isaac. 1614. *De rebus sacris et ecclesiasticis exercitationes XVI.* London.

Colish, Marcia L. 1992. "Stoicism in the New Testament: An Essay in Historiography." *ANRW* II.26.1:334–79.

Conzelmann, Hans. 1965. "Paulus und die Weisheit." *NTS* 12:231–44.

———. 1966. "Luke's Place in the Development of Early Christianity."

In *Studies in Luke-Acts: Essays Presented in Honor of Paul Schubert,* ed. Leander E. Keck and J. Louis Martin, 298–316. Nashville and New York: Abingdon.

Cotter, Wendy J. 1993. *"Our Politeuma Is in Heaven:* The Meaning of Phil. 3.17–21." In *Origins and Method: Towards a New Understanding of Judaism and Christianity. Essays in Honour of John C. Hurd,* ed. Bradley H. McLean, 92–104. JSNTSup 86. Sheffield: JSOT Press.

Countryman, L. William. 1977. "Patrons and Officers in Club and Church." In *SBL 1977 Seminar Papers,* ed. P. J. Achtemeier, 135–43. SBLASP 11. Missoula: Scholars Press.

Danker, Frederick W. 1982. *Benefactor: Epigraphic Study of a Graeco-Roman and New Testament Semantic Field.* St. Louis: Clayton.

———. 1992. "Associations, Clubs, Thiasoi." *ABD* 1:501–3.

de Lacy, Phillip H. 1948. "Lucretius and the History of Epicureanism." *TAPA* 79:12–23.

de Rossi, Giovanni Battista. 1864–77. *La Roma sotteranea cristiana.* Rome: Cromo-litografia Pontificia.

De Witt, Norman W. 1936. "Organization and Procedure in Epicurean Groups." *CP* 31:205–11.

———. 1944–45. "Epicurianism and Christianity." *University of Toronto Quarterly* 14:250–55.

———. 1954a. *Epicurus and His Philosophy.* Minneapolis: University of Minnesota Press.

———. 1954b. *St. Paul and Epicurus.* Minneapolis: University of Minnesota Press.

Dombrowski, B. W. 1966. *"HYḤD* in IQS and *to koinon:* An Instance of Early Greek and Jewish Synthesis." *HTR* 59:293–307.

Donfried, Karl P. 1985. "The Cults of Thessalonica and the Thessalonian Correspondence." *NTS* 31:336–56.

———. 1993. "2 Thessalonians and the Church of Thessalonica." In *Origins and Method: Towards a New Understanding of Judaism and Christianity. Essays in Honour of John C. Hurd,* ed. Bradley H. McLean, 128–44. JSNTSup 86. Sheffield: JSOT Press.

Edson, Charles. 1940. "Macedonica." *HSCP* 51:125–36.

———. 1948. "Cults of Thessalonica (Macedonica III)." *HTR* 41:153–204.

Engberg-Pedersen, Troels, ed. 1995. *Paul in His Hellenistic Context.* Minneapolis: Fortress.

————. 1995. "Stoicism in Philippians." In *Paul in His Hellenistic Context,* ed. Troels Engberg-Pedersen, 256–90. Minneapolis: Fortress.

Feldman, Louis H. 1986. "The Omnipresence of the God-Fearers." BARev 12/5:58–69.

Ferguson, Everett. 1987. *Backgrounds of Early Christianity.* Grand Rapids: Eerdmans.

Filson, Floyd. 1939. "The Significance of the Early House Churches." *JBL* 58:109–12.

Fisher, Nicholas R. E. 1988. "Greek Associations, Symposia, and Clubs." In *Civilization of the Ancient Mediterranean: Greece and Rome,* ed. Michael Grant and Rachel Kitzinger, 1167–97. New York: Charles Scribner's Sons.

Fitzgerald, John T., ed. 1996. *Friendship, Flattery, and Frankness of Speech: Studies on Friendship in the New Testament World.* NovTSup 82. Leiden/New York/Köln: Brill.

Gager, John G. 1975. *Kingdom and Community: The Social World of Early Christianity.* Englewood Cliffs, NJ: Prentice-Hall.

Garnsey, Peter, and Richard Saller. 1987. *The Roman Empire: Economy, Society and Culture.* London: Duckworth.

Gaston, Lloyd. 1993. "Pharisaic Problems." In *Approaches to Ancient Judaism,* New Series 3., ed. Jacob Neusner, 85–100. Atlanta: Scholars Press.

Georgi, Dieter. 1986. *The Opponents of Paul in Second Corinthians.* Philadelphia: Fortress.

————. 1995. "The Early Church: Internal Jewish Migration or New Religion." *HTR* 88:35–68.

Gill, David W. J. 1994. "Achaia." In *The Book of Acts in Its First Century Setting 2: The Book of Acts in Its Graeco-Roman Setting,* ed. David W. J. Gill and Conrad Gempf, 433–53. Grand Rapids and Carlisle: Eerdmans and Paternoster.

Glad, Clarence E. 1995. *Paul and Philodemus: Adaptability in Epicurean and Early Christian Psychagogy.* NovTSup 81. Leiden/New York/Köln: Brill.

Goodman, Martin. 1992. "Jewish Proselytizing in the First Century." In

The Jews Among Pagans and Christians in the Roman Empire, ed. Judith Lieu, John North, and Tessa Rajak, 53–78. London and New York: Routledge.

———. 1994. *Mission and Conversion: Proselytizing in the Religious History of the Roman Empire.* Oxford: Clarendon.

Gordon, Arthur E. 1983. *Illustrated Introduction to Latin Epigraphy.* Berkeley and Los Angeles: University of California Press.

Goulder, Michael D. 1992. "Silas in Thessalonica." *JSNT* 48:87–106.

Guerra, Anthony J. 1995. *Romans and the Apologetic Tradition: The Purpose, Genre and Audience of Paul's Letter.* SNTSMS 81. Cambridge: Cambridge University Press.

Hanson, K. C. 1989. "The Herodians and Mediterranean Kinship. Part 2: Marriage and Divorce." *Biblical Theology Bulletin* 19:142–51.

Hardy, E. G. 1906. *Studies in Roman History* 1. London and New York: Sonnenschein and MacMillan.

Harnack, Adolf von. 1887. "On the Origin of the Christian Ministry." *Expositor* 3/5:321–43.

Hatch, Edwin. 1881. *The Organization of Early Christian Churches: Eight Lectures.* Bampton Lectures. London: Rivingtons.

———. 1891. *The Influence of Greek Ideas on Christianity.* The Hibbert Lectures, 1888. London: Williams and Norgate. (Reprinted Peabody: Hendrickson, 1995).

Heinrici, Georg. 1876. "Die Christengemeinden Korinths und die religiösen Genossenschaften der Griechen." *ZWT* 19:465–526.

———. 1877. "Zur Geschichte der Anfänge paulinischer Gemeinden." *ZWT* 20:89–130.

———. 1881. "Zum genossenschaftlichen Charakter der paulinischen Christengemeinden." *TSK* 54:505–24.

———. 1896. *Der erste Brief an die Korinther.* Kritisch-exegetischer Kommentar überdas Neue Testament 5. 8th edition. Göttingen: Vandenhoeck & Ruprecht.

Hemer, Colin J. 1983. "The Cities of Revelation." *NewDocs* 3:51–58.

Hock, Ronald F. 1978. "Paul's Tentmaking and the Problem of His Social Class." *JBL* 97:555–64.

———. 1979. "The Workshop as a Social Setting for Paul's Missionary Preaching." *CBQ* 41:438–50.

———. 1980. *The Social Context of Paul's Ministry: Tentmaking and Apostleship.* Philadelphia: Fortress.

Horsley, G. H. R. 1982. "The Purple Trade, and the Status of Lydia of Thyatira." *NewDocs* 2:25–32.

Inwood, Brad, L. P. Gerson, and D. S. Hutchinson, eds. 1994. *The Epicurus Reader: Selected Writings and Testimonia.* Indianapolis and Cambridge: Hackett.

Jeffers, James S. 1991. *Conflict at Rome: Social Order and Hierarchy in Early Christianity.* Minneapolis: Fortress.

Jeremias, J. 1958. *Jesus' Promise to the Nations: The Franz Delitzsch Lectures for 1953.* London: SMC.

Jewett, Robert. 1986. *The Thessalonian Correspondence: Pauline Rhetoric and Millenarian Piety.* Foundations and Facets. Philadelphia: Fortress.

Jones, A. H. M. 1955. "The Economic Life of the Towns of the Roman Empire." In *La Ville: Deuxième partie: Institutions économiques et sociales,* vol 2., ed. Jean Firenne, 161–94. Recueils de la Société Jean Bodin 7. Brussels: Editions de la Libraire Éncyclopédique.

Josaitis, Norman F. 1971. *Edwin Hatch and Early Church Order.* Gembloux: Éditions J.Duculot.

Judge, E. A. 1960a. "The Early Christians as a Scholastic Community." *JRH* 111:4–15.

———. 1960b. *The Social Pattern of Christian Groups in the First Century: Some Prolegomena to the Study of New Testament Ideas of Social Obligation.* London: Tyndale.

———. 1972. "St. Paul and Classical Society." *JAC* 15:19–36.

———. 1980. "The Social Identity of the First Christians: A Question of Method in Religious History." *JRH* 11:201–17.

Juster, G. 1914. *Les Juifs dans l'empire romain.* Reprint. New York: Burt Franklin.

Kee, Howard Clark. 1990. "The Transformation of the Synagogue After 70 C.E.: Its Import for Early Christianity." *NTS* 36:1–24.

———. 1994. "The Changing Meaning of Synagogue: A Response to Richard Oster." *NTS* 40:281–83.

———. 1995a. "Defining the First-Century C.E. Synagogue: Problems and Progress." *NTS* 41:481–500.

———. 1995b. *Who Are the People of God? Early Christian Models of Community.* New Haven and London: Yale University Press.

Kennedy, H. A. A. 1913. *St. Paul and the Mystery-religions*. London: Hodder & Stoughton.

Klauck, Hans-Josef. 1981a. "Die Hausgemeinde als Lebensform im Urchristentum." *MTZ* 32:1–15.

———. 1981b. *Hausgemeinde und Hauskirche im frühen Christentum.* Stuttgarter Bibelstudien 103. Stuttgart: Katholisches Bibelwerk.

———. 1982. *Herrenmahl und hellenistischer Kult: Eine religionsgeschichtliche Untersuchung zum ersten Korintherbrief.* Neutestamentliche Abhandlungen 15. Münster: Aschendorff.

———. 1992. *Gemeinde zwischen Haus und Stadt: Kirche bei Paulus.* Freiburg/Basel/Wien:Herder.

Kloppenborg, John S. 1988. *Q Parallels: Synopsis, Critical Notes, and Concordance*. Sonoma, CA: Polebridge Press.

———. 1993a. "Edwin Hatch, Churches and Collegia." In *Origins and Method: Towards a New Understanding of Judaism and Christianity. Essays in Honour of John C. Hurd,* ed. Bradley H. McLean, 212–38. JSNTSup 86. Sheffield: JSOT Press.

———. 1993b. "*Philadelphia, Theodidaktos* and the Dioscuri: Rhetorical Engagement in 1 Thessalonians 4.9–12." *NTS* 39:265–89.

———. 1996a. "Collegia and *Thiasoi:* Issues in Function, Taxonomy and Membership." In *Voluntary Associations in the Graeco-Roman World,* ed. John S. Kloppenborg and Steven G. Wilson, 16–30. London and New York: Routledge.

———. 1996b. "Egalitarianism in the Myth and Rhetoric of Pauline Churches." In *Reimagining Christian Origins: A Colloquium Honoring Burton L. Mack,* ed. Elizabeth A. Castelli and Hal Taussig, 247–63. Valley Forge: Trinity Press International.

Knox, John. 1987. *Chapters in a Life of Paul.* 2nd edition. Macon: Mercer University Press.

Kraabel, A. Thomas. 1981. "The Disappearance of the 'God-Fearers.'" *Numen* 28:113–26 (Reprinted in Overman and MacLennan 1992:119–30).

———. 1994. "Immigrants, Exiles, Expatriates, and Missionaries." In *Religious Propaganda and Missionary Competition in the New Testament World: Essays Honoring Dieter Georgi,* ed. Lukas Bormann, Kelly Del Tredici, and Angela Standhartinger, 71-88. NovTSup 74. Leiden: Brill.

Lease, Gary. 1980. "Mithraism and Christianity: Borrowings and Transformations." *ANRW* II.23.2:1306–32.

Liebenam, W. 1890. *Zur Geschichte und organisation des römischen Vereinswesens: Drei Untersuchungen.* Leipzig: Teubner.

Lieu, Judith M. 1994. "Do God-Fearers Make Good Christians?" *In Crossing the Boundaries: Essays in Biblical Interpretation in Honour of Michael D. Goulder,* ed. Stanley E. Porter, Paul Joyce, and David E. Orton, 329–45. Biblical Interpretation Series 8. Leiden/New York/Köln: Brill.

Lobeck, C. A. 1829. *Aglaophamus, sive de theologiae mysticae Graecorum causis, idemque poetrarum Orphicorum dispersas.* 2 vols. Königsberg.

Loisy, Alfred. 1911–12. "The Christian Mystery." *Hibbert Journal* 10:45–64.

———. 1914. *Les mystères païens et le mystère chrétien.* Paris: Emile Nourry.

Lüdemann, Gerd. 1987. *Early Christianity According to the Traditions in Acts: A Commentary.* Minneapolis: Fortress.

McKnight, Scot. 1991. *A Light Among the Gentiles: Jewish Missionary Activity in the Second Temple Period.* Minneapolis: Fortress.

McLean, Bradley H. 1993. "The Agrippinilla Inscription: Religious Associations and Early Church Formation." In *Origins and Method: Towards a New Understanding of Judaism and Christianity. Essays in Honour of John C. Hurd,* ed. Bradley H. McLean, 239–70. JSNTSup 86. Sheffield: JSOT Press.

MacLennan, Robert S., and A. T. Kraabel. 1986. "The God-Fearers—A Literary and Theological Invention." *BARev* 12/5:46–53, 64. (Reprinted in Overman and MacLennan 1992:131–44).

MacMullen, Ramsay, and Eugene N. Lane, eds. 1992. *Paganism and Christianity 100–425 C.E.: A Sourcebook.* Minneapolis: Fortress.

Maccoby, Hyam. 1986. *The Mythmaker: Paul and the Invention of Christianity.* New York: Harper & Row.

———. 1991. *Paul and Hellenism.* Valley Forge: Trinity Press International.

Malherbe, Abraham J. 1983. *Social Aspects of Early Christianity.* 2nd edition. Philadelphia: Fortress.

————. 1987. *Paul and the Thessalonians: The Philosophic Tradition of Pastoral Care.* Philadelphia: Fortress.

————. 1989a. "Graeco-Roman Religion and Philosophy and the New Testament." In *The New Testament and Its Modern Interpreters,* Eldon Jay Epp, and George MacRae, 1–26. Atlanta: Scholars Press.

————. 1989b. *Paul and the Popular Philosophers.* Minneapolis: Fortress.

————. 1989c. "Paul: Hellenistic Philosopher or Christian Pastor?" In *Paul and the Popular Philosophers,* Abraham J. Malherbe, 67–77. Minneapolis: Fortress.

————. 1990. "Pastoral Care in the Thessalonian Church." *NTS* 36:375–91.

————. 1992. "Hellenistic Moralists and the New Testament." *ANRW* II.26.1:267–333.

Marcus, Ralph. 1952. "Philo, Josephus and the Dead Sea *Yahad.*" JBL 71:207–9.

Marrou, Henri. 1955. *A History of Education in Antiquity.* New York: Sheed and Ward.

Martens, John W. 1994. "Romans 2:14–16: A Stoic Reading." *NTS* 40:55–67.

Martin, Luther H. 1987. *Hellenistic Religions: An Introduction.* New York and Oxford: Oxford University Press.

Mason, Steve N. 1996. "*Philosophiai:* Greco-Roman, Jewish, and Christian." In *Voluntary Associations in the Graeco-Roman World,* ed. John S. Kloppenborg and Stephen G. Wilson, 31–58. London and New York: Routledge.

Meeks, Wayne A. 1980. "The Urban Environment of Pauline Christianity." In *SBL 1980 Seminar Papers,* ed. P. J. Achtemeier, 113–22. SBLASP 19. Chico: Scholars Press.

————. 1983. *The First Urban Christians: The Social World of the Apostle Paul.* New Haven: Yale University Press.

————. 1985. "Breaking Away: Three New Testament Pictures of Christianity's Separation From the Jewish Communities." In *'To See Ourselves As Others See Us': Christians, Jews, 'Others' in Late Antiquity,* eds. Jacob Neusner and Ernest S. Frerichs, 93–115. Scholars Press Studies in the Humanities. Chico: Scholars Press.

———. 1986. *The Moral World of the First Christians.* LEC 6. Philadelphia: Westminster.

———. 1993. *The Origins of Christian Morality: The First Two Centuries.* New Haven: Yale University Press.

Metzger, Bruce M. 1968. "Methodology in the Study of the Mystery Religions and Early Christianity." In *Historical and Literary Studies: Pagan, Jewish and Christian,* Bruce M. Metzger, 1–24. New Testament Tools and Studies 8. Grand Rapids: Eerdmans.

———. 1984. "A Classified Bibliography of the Graeco-Roman Mystery Religions 1924–1973 with a supplement 1978–1979." *ANRW* II.17.3:1259–423.

Meyer, Marvin W. 1992. "Mystery Religions." *ABD* 4:941–45.

Mommsen, Theodore. 1843. *De collegiis et sodaliciis Romanorum: Accedit inscriptio lanuvina.* Kiel: Libraria Schwersiana.

Murphy-O'Connor, Jerome. 1992. "Lots of God-Fearers? *Theosebeis* in the Aphrodisias Inscription." *RB* 99:418–24.

Nock, A. D. 1933. *Conversion: The Old and the New in Religion from Alexander the Great to Augustine of Hippo.* Oxford: Oxford University Press.

———. 1972a. "Early Gentile Christianity and its Hellenistic Background." In *Essays on Religion and the Ancient World,* ed. Zeph Stewart, 49–133. Oxford: Clarendon.

———. 1972b. "The Genius of Mithraism." In *Essays on Religion and the Ancient World,* ed. Zeph Stewart, 452–58. Oxford: Clarendon.

———. 1972c. "Hellenistic Mysteries and Christian Sacraments." In *Essays on Religion in the Ancient World,* ed. Zeph Stewart, 791–820. Oxford: Clarendon.

———. 1972d. "'Son of God' in Pauline and Hellenistic Thought." In *Essays on Religion in the Ancient World,* ed. Zeph Stewart, 928–39. Oxford: Clarendon.

———. 1972e. "The Vocabulary of the New Testament." In *Essays on Religion in the Ancient World,* ed. Zeph Stewart, 341–47. Oxford: Clarendon.

Osiek, Carolyn. 1992. *What Are They Saying About the Social Setting of the New Testament?* 2nd edition. New York and Mahwah, NJ: Paulist.

Oster, Richard E. 1993. "Supposed Anachronism in Luke-Acts' Use of *synagōguē.*" *NTS* 39:178–208.

Overman, J. Andrew. 1992. "The God-Fearers: Some Neglected Features." In *Diaspora Jews and Judaism: Essays in Honor of, and in Dialogue with, A. Thomas Kraabel,* ed. J. Andrew Overman and Robert S. MacLennan, 145–52. South Florida Studies in the History of Judaism 41. Atlanta: Scholars Press. (Reprint of *JSNT* 32 [1988] 17–26).

Overman, J. Andrew and Robert S. MacLennan, eds. 1992. *Diaspora Jews and Judaism: Essays in Honor of, and in Dialogue with, A. Thomas Kraabel.* South Florida Studies in the History of Judaism 41. Atlanta: Scholars Press.

Petersen, Joan M. 1969. "House-Churches in Rome." *VC* 23:264–72.

Radin, Max. 1910. *The Legislation of the Greeks and Romans on Corporations.* Columbia University: Tuttle, Morehouse & Taylor.

Rahner, Hugo. 1963. "Christian Mystery and the Pagan Mysteries." In *Pagan and Christian Mysteries: Papers from the Eranos Yearbooks,* ed. Joseph Cambell, 146–210. New York: Harper.

Rajak, Tessa. 1985. "Jews and Christians as Groups in a Pagan World." In *'To See Ourselves As Others See Us': Christians, Jews, 'Others' in Late Antiquity,* ed. Jacob Neusner and Ernest S. Frerichs, 247–62. Scholars Press Studies in the Humanities. Chico: Scholars Press.

Rajak, Tessa, and D. Noy. 1993. "*Archisynagōgoi:* Office, Title and Status in the Greco-Roman World." *JRS* 83:75–93.

Ramish, Sandra Walker. 1996. "Greco-Roman Voluntary Associations and the Damascus Document: A Sociological Analysis." In *Voluntary Associations in the Graeco-Roman World,* ed. John S. Kloppenborg and Stephen G. Wilson, 128–45. London and New York: Routledge.

Reitzenstein, Richard. 1978. *Hellenistic Mystery-Religions: Their Basic Ideas and Significance.* PTM 18. Pittsburgh: Pickwick.

Renan, Ernest. 1866. *The Apostles.* New York: Carleton.

Reynolds, Joyce M. and Robert Tannenbaum. 1987. *Jews and God-fearers at Aphrodisias: Greek Inscriptions With Commentary.* Proceedings of the Cambridge Philological Society, Supplementary 12. Cambridge: Cambridge Philological Society.

Richardson, G. Peter. 1996. "Early Synagogues as Collegia in the

Diaspora and Palestine." In *Voluntary Associations in the Graeco-Roman World,* ed. John S. Kloppenborg and Stephen G. Wilson, 90–109. London and New York: Routledge.

Riches, John K. 1993. *A Century of New Testament Study.* Cambridge: Lutterworth.

Roberts, C. H., T. C. Skeat, and A. D. Nock. 1936. "The Guild of Zeus Hypsistos." *HTR* 29:39–88.

Sampley, J. Paul. 1980. *Pauline Partnership in Christ.* Philadelphia: Fortress.

Schmeller, Thomas. 1995. *Hierarchie und Egalität: Eine sozialgeschichtliche Untersuchung paulinischer Gemeinden und griechisch-römischer Vereine.* Stuttgarter Bibelstudien 162. Stuttgart: Katholisches Bibelwerk.

Schmid, Wolfgang. 1962. "Epikur." *RAC* 5:681–819.

Scroggs, Robin. 1980. "The Sociological Interpretation of the New Testament: The Present State of Research." *NTS* 26:164–79.

Segal, Alan F. 1990. *Paul the Convert: The Apostolate and Apostasy of Saul the Pharisee.* New Haven and London: Yale University Press.

Simpson, A. D. 1941. "Epicureans, Christians, Atheists in the Second Century." *TAPA* 72:372–81.

Smallwood, E. Mary. 1976. *The Jews Under Roman Rule.* Studies in Judaism in Late Antiquity 20. Leiden: Brill.

Smith, Jonathan Z. 1978. "Too Much Kingdom / Too Little Community." *Zygon* 13:123–30.

————. 1990. *Drudgery Divine: On the Comparison of Early Christianities and the Religions of Late Antiquity.* Chicago: University of Chicago Press.

Stambaugh, John E., and David L. Balch. 1986. *The New Testament in Its Social Environment.* LEC 2. Philadelphia: Westminster.

Stowers, Stanley K. 1981. *The Diatribe and Paul's Letter to the Romans.* SBLDS 57. Chico: Scholars Press.

————. 1984. "Social Status, Public Speaking and Private Teaching." *NovT* 26:59–82.

————. 1988. "The Diatribe." In *Greco-Roman Literature and the New Testament: Selected Forms and Genres,* ed. David E. Aune, 71–83. SBLSBS 21. Atlanta: Scholars Press.

Tannenbaum, Robert F. 1986. "Jews and God-Fearers in the Holy City of Aphrodite." *BARev* 12/5:54–57.

Teeple, Howard M. 1988. "How Mithra Won the West." In *SBL 1988 Seminar Papers,* ed. D. J. Lull, 312–17. SBLASP 27. Atlanta: Scholars Press.

———. 1992. *How Did Christianity Really Begin? A Historical-Archaeological Approach.* Evanston, IL: Religion and Ethics Institute.

Tod, Marcus N. 1932. *Sidelights on Greek History: Three Lectures on the Light Thrown By Greek Inscriptions on the Life and Thought of the Ancient World.* Oxford: Blackwell.

Trebilco, Paul R. 1994. "Asia." In *The Book of Acts in Its First Century Setting 2: The Book of Acts in Its Graeco-Roman Setting,* ed. David W. J. Gill and Conrad Gempf, 291–362. Grand Rapids and Carlisle: Eerdmans and Paternoster.

Urman, Dan, and Paul V. M. Flesher. 1995. "Ancient Synagogues: A Reader's Guide." In *Ancient Synagogues: Historical Analysis and Archaeological Discovery.* Vol. 1., ed. Dan Urman and Paul V. M. Flesher, xvii–xxxvii. SPB 47/1. Leiden/New York/Köln: Brill.

Wagner, Günther. 1967. *Pauline Baptism and the Pagan Mysteries: The Problem of the Pauline Doctrine of Baptism in Romans VI,1–11, in the Light of its Religio-Historical 'Parallels'.* Edinburgh and London: Oliver & Boyd.

Waltzing, J.-P. 1895, 1896, 1899, 1900. *Étude Historique sur les corporations Professionnelles chez les Romains depuis les origines jusqu'a la chute de l'Empire d'Occident.* 4 Vols. Mémoire couronne par l'Academie royale des Sciences, des Lettres et des Beaux-Arts de Belgique. Louvain: Peeters.

Wedderburn, A. J. M. 1982. "Paul and the Hellenistic Mystery-Cults: On Posing the Right Questions." In *La Soteriologia Dei Culti Orientali Nell' Impero Romano: Atti del Colloquio Internazionale su La soteriologia dei culti orientali nell' Impero Romano,* ed. Ugo Bianchi and Maarten J. Vermasern, 817–33. EPRO 92. Leiden: Brill.

———. 1983. "Hellenistic Christian Traditions in Romans 6?" *NTS* 29:337–55.

———. 1987a. *Baptism and Resurrection: Studies in Pauline Theology Against Its Graeco-Roman Background.* WUNT 44. Tübingen: Mohr (Siebeck).

————. 1987b. "The Soteriology of the Mysteries and Pauline Baptismal Theology." *NovT* 29:53–72.

Weinfeld, Moshe. 1986. *The Organizational Pattern and the Penal Code of the Qumran Sect: A Comparison With Guilds and Religious Associations of the Hellenistic Period.* NovT et orbis antiquus 2. Göttingen: Vandenhoeck & Ruprecht.

Whelan, Caroline F. 1993. *"Amica Pauli:* The Role of Phoebe in the Early Church." *JSNT* 49:67–85.

White, L. Michael. 1990. *Building God's House in the Roman World: Architectural Adaptation Among Pagans, Jews and Christians.* ASOR Library of Biblical and Near Eastern Archaeology. Baltimore: Johns Hopkins University Press.

Wiens, Devon H. 1980. "Mystery Concepts in Primitive Christianity and in its Environment." *ANRW* II.23.2:1248–84.

Wilcox, Max. 1981. "The 'God-Fearers' in Acts—A Reconsideration." *JSNT* 13:102–22.

Wilken, Robert L. 1971. "Collegia, Philosophical Schools and Theology." In *The Catacombs and the Colosseum: The Roman Empire as the Setting of Primitive Christianity,* ed. Stephen Benko and John J. O'Rourke, 268–91. Valley Forge: Judson.

————. 1984. *The Christians as the Romans Saw Them.* New Haven and London: Yale University Press.

Wilson, Thomas. 1927. *St. Paul and Paganism.* Edinburgh: T. & T. Clark.

Winter, Bruce W. 1994. *Seek the Welfare of the City: Christians as Benefactors and Citizens.* First-Century Christians in the Graeco-Roman World. Grand Rapids and Carlisle: Eerdmans and Paternoster.

Witherington III, Ben. 1994. *Friendship and Finances in Philippi: The Letter of Paul to the Philippians.* The New Testament in Context. Valley Forge: Trinity Press International.

Witt, R. E. 1966a. "The Importance of Isis for the Fathers." *Studia Patristica* 8:135–45.

————. 1966b. "Isis-Hellas." *Proceedings of the Cambridge Philological Society* 192 (n.s. 12):48–69.

————. 1971. *Isis in the Graeco-Roman World.* Aspects of Greek and Roman Life. London: Thames and Hudson.

Suggestions
for Further Study

Barton, S. C., and G. H. R. Horsley. 1981. "A Hellenistic Cult Group and the New Testament Churches." *JAC* 24:7–41.

This lengthy article provides a detailed comparison of the regulations of a private voluntary association found in *SIG*^{3} 985 and the Christian churches. While the authors find many points of similarity, they also highlight the differences. For those not familiar with the inscriptions of the voluntary associations, this article will provide a solid base from which to start. Along with their analysis the authors provide an English translation of the inscription.

Branick, Vincent. 1989. *The House Church in Paul.* Zacchaeus Studies: New Testament. Wilmington, DE: Michael Glazier.

A good general introduction to the concept of the household in antiquity and its significance for understanding Christian community formation.

Engberg-Pedersen, Troels, ed. 1995. *Paul in His Hellenistic Context.* Minneapolis: Fortress.

A number of essays in this fine collection provide a solid exegetical perspective on Paul's relationship to the philosophical schools and the mystery religions. Other essays investigate Paul's Jewish background while still others make some broader methodological observations. We have summarized Aune 1995; Alexander 1995; Betz 1995; Borgen 1995; Engberg-Pedersen 1995.

Goodman, Martin. 1994. *Mission and Conversion: Proselytizing in the Religious History of the Roman Empire.* Oxford: Clarendon.

An excellent analysis of Jewish proselytisim in the first century. In the process of the study, he also investigates supposed missionary activities in philosophical schools and the mystery religions. He concludes that there is little evidence for a tendency towards missionary efforts in any of these groups. The idea of a universal plan to evangelize the world originates with Christianity itself.

Judge, E. A. 1960. *The Social Pattern of Christian Groups in the First Century: Some Prolegomena to the Study of New Testament Ideas of Social Obligation.* London: Tyndale.

One of the earliest among recent voices to advocate and undertake the study of Christian social identity in the context of its contemporary society, this short book still repays careful reading.

Kee, Howard Clark. 1995. *Who Are the People of God? Early Christian Models of Community.* New Haven and London: Yale University Press.

The attempt to understand various early Christian communities from five Jewish community models and Jewish texts from outside the Hebrew Bible provides a good introduction to the interaction of various forms of early Judaism with various branches of Christianity as they parted ways.

Kloppenborg, John S. and Stephen G. Wilson. 1996. *Voluntary Associations in the Graeco-Roman World.* London and New York: Routledge.

A collection of essays that bring together the best of modern studies of voluntary associations while summarizing much of what has been done in the past. Most of the essays outline the use of voluntary associations in understanding one or more of the various ancient groups such as philosophical schools, various forms of Judaism (Philo, synagogues, Qumran), and early Christianity.

Malherbe, Abraham J. 1987. *Paul and the Thessalonians: The Philosophic Tradition of Pastoral Care.* Philadelphia: Fortress.

A study of how Paul founded, shaped and nurtured his Christian community at Thessalonica as it is reflected in his earliest letter, 1 Thessalonians. Malherbe's wide reading of Greco-Roman philosophical literature allows him to draw many parallels between Paul's pastoral approach and that of the popular moral philosophers. The book provides a good introduction to the moral philosophers while showing their relevance for the study of early Christianity.

Meeks, Wayne A. 1983. *The First Urban Christians: The Social World of the Apostle Paul.* New Haven: Yale University Press.

While only a few pages of this book summarize various possible community analogies for early Christianity (pp. 74–84), it is essential reading for anyone interested in the urban environment in which Christianity flourished. This is primarily a sociological study of the status and interaction of the members of Paul's communities.

Metzger, Bruce M. 1968. "Methodology in the Study of the Mystery Religions and Early Christianity." In *Historical and Literary Studies: Pagan, Jewish and Christian,* Bruce M. Metzger, 1–24. New Testament Tools and Studies 8. Grand Rapids: Eerdmans.

This essay provides a brief overview of the history of scholarship on the comparison of Christianity and the mystery religions and then offers methodological considerations for those pursuing the question further. While not nearly as comprehensive nor as insightful as Smith 1990, it will provide the beginning student with a profitable starting point.

Nock, A. D. 1972. *Essays on Religion and the Ancient World,* ed. Zeph Stewart. Oxford: Clarendon.

This two-volume collection of many of Nock's more important essays and book reviews provides the reader with a comprehensive resource of material for use in the study of ancient Christianity in its Hellenistic context. Since many of Nock's longer essays are reproduced here, any one of them will provide the reader with a good introduction to Nock's approach, especially "Early Gentile Christianity and Its Hellenistic Background" (pp. 49–133).

Overman, J. Andrew and Robert S. MacLennan, eds. 1992. *Diaspora Jews and Judaism: Essays in Honor of, and in Dialogue with, A. Thomas Kraabel.* South Florida Studies in the History of Judaism 41. Atlanta: Scholars Press.

A collection of new and reprinted essays. Half of the twenty-two essays are written by A. T. Kraable (with one cowritten) while the remaining half are written by his colleagues in response to his arguments and conclusions. This book provides a solid overview of, among many topics, the nature and roles of the synagogues in the Diaspora, the evidence for and against the existence of the "God-fearers," and the interaction between Judaism and the larger Greco-Roman culture. We have summarized Kraabel 1981, MacLennan and Kraabel 1986, and Overman 1992, all of which appear in this volume.

Smith, Jonathan Z. 1990. *Drudgery Divine: On the Comparison of Early Christianities and the Religions of Late Antiquity.* Chicago: University of Chicago Press.

One of the most important books to be published in this decade on methodology in the study of early Christianity in its context. Smith highlights a number of ways in which previous scholars have introduced biases into their investigations (intentionally or not) which have adversely affected their conclusions. It is hoped that his argument for comparing data analogically will bear much fruit in the future. This book is definitely worth reading and rereading.

Other Books in This Series